BUSINESS PR
HONOR GOD; WORLDWIDE!
Startups, Operations, Successes and Failures.
By Edward S. Rowse

This book is a work of non-fiction. Unless otherwise noted, the author makes no explicit guarantees as to the accuracy of the information contained in this book. Because of the dynamic nature of the Internet, any web addresses or links contained in this book may have changed & may no longer be valid. The views expressed in this work are solely those of the author.

TABLE OF CONTENTS

PREFACE

If you would like to start your own business, but have no idea where to start, then read this book. If you have a business and would like to shed the burdens that it brings, then read this book. If you would like to improve your business to a more profitable and satisfying one, then read this book. If you would like to change your business from what it is today to something else, then read this book. If you would like to be a much more knowledgeable employee of the company for whom you work, then read this book! The information contained benefits at least three categories of readers:

1. People who wish to go into business themselves, become entrepreneurs, anywhere in the world, crossing cultural lines if needed.
2. People who wish to help others become established in a business of their own, and
3. People who wish to use these principles to become more valuable employees in the company in which they work

Business Guidance

The birth rate for new businesses, startups and entrepreneurships is high, and so is the mortality rate. I have talked with people the world over, and listen to many stories of false starts, "I wish I had never", bankruptcies and disappointments, and have become burdened for people who have these experiences. My own journey working within a large corporation was a 37 year stretch of generally good experiences, falling back on them as my venture capitalist and delivering good results. I learned a lot during this time and will be forever grateful for that. It's like comparing a happy childhood to one that wasn't so fortunate. I have pondered the reasons why new business failure rate is so high, and why older businesses linger for a long time and then fade away in ignominy. I have come to the conclusion that there are many reasons, some interrelated and some not. The purpose of this book is to offer some advice about how to anticipate what could happen to you before it happens and to ward off the possibility of money and time poorly spent and to prevent disappointment or to help your business thrive and deliver the results you want.

Two things are important. The first is your relationship with God and the resultant definition of success. What is success, in your mind? What are you willing to do to attain success? How can you reach a point when you can look back on your life with satisfaction and knowing that you have achieved what God designed you for? That may not be monetary wealth, but something quite different, but immensely satisfying. If it is monetary wealth, are you happy to give it away for the kingdom of God? Do you find joy in giving away much of what you have earned? Joy may not come in the form of monetary wealth, but the satisfaction of providing many jobs for others, and having an impact on the lives of others to them and their families. For others, joy and satisfaction may come in the achievement of something that others said you couldn't do. As Walt Disney famously said "doing the impossible is fun."

The second thing that is important is being able to share what you know with others, especially the younger generation. I have spent my 20 years of retirement, teaching classes in Ukraine, the USA, Vietnam, China, Peru, Cote d'Ivoire and many other places in the world. I find joy in talking with university students as well as third graders. There, you look into the eyes of the future. I want to share Christ's love with them, and to impart to them the experiences I have been privileged to have in life. Because of Christ who set me on the proper path as a very young man, and because I obeyed Him and held to His principles, and put Him first, my life has been successful. Final success will be when He says to me "well done, good and faithful servant."

This is what compels me to share my life with you. I do not want you to fail. I do not want you to waste your life chasing unrealities. I want you to succeed in all that you do. This book is an expression of that wish. I hope you heed it's advice

Ed's Christian Testimony

I was not a Christian for the first 21 years of life. I went through schools, and then University, studied engineering, and got a good job. But my life was empty and I lacked the love that I wanted. I went to a church to have a little fun, with no intention of finding God. But there, God found me. I listened to the message from the Bible with great interest, and came to realize that I was a sinner, lost and with no hope of heaven. I learned that Jesus loved me enough to die for my sins, and that his blood was shed on the cross for me. At first opportunity, I invited Jesus to come into my heart and take full control of me. That took place on July 7,1963. My life began to change, and truly the old passed away, and my life became new. Old habits and old attitudes disappeared or changed. Jesus gave me a new heart and began to show me His will for my life. I became aware of the gifts He had given me, and by His Holy Spirit, He gave me the ability to use them. I love my family consisting of my wife Suzanne and our 55 years together, and our three children, Doug, Julie and Jennifer, and our eight grandchildren, who all walk with the Lord. I also thank Him for my church family and many good friends who give me sound, godly advice. It is my purpose to do whatever my Lord wants for the rest of my life. Jesus rose from the cross and lives in heaven today, but He is coming again soon, and there is much for me to do to share the Good News with as many as possible in the time I have left. His words to me "well done, my good and faithful servant" is the only reward I seek. Praise be the Name of the Lord!

INTRODUCTION

This book has several purposes. One is to use the Bible as a way of guiding us through wiser choices which may impact our business and our clientele. It is the author's belief that God wants to be our senior partner in our business and therefore His advice and counsel is essential. How can we honor God in our business?

Another purpose is to take this message around the world, interacting with many cultures, and applying these universal principles. Every culture is fascinating, and ways of doing business are different and must be understood and respected. This book contains the kind of guidance which could be applied anywhere in the world, whether it is someone setting up a business within their own culture, or someone from one culture attempting to do business in another one. Some of the reference books contain more detailed information about other cultures.

Still another purpose is to start at the ground level and to provide a very practical guide. This is not a book about macro or micro economic theory or the stock market. This book will give you no guidance about shareholders rate of return, investor's rate of return, net present value calculations or the time value of money. It will not provide you with a course suitable for an MBA. It will not talk about international currency manipulations or rates of exchange. Rather it is a compendium of the author's personal experience and learnings as an employee of a very large chemical company, many observations about other businesses over many years in many countries, and personal experience as a small business owner. My purpose can be simply stated: "I have learned a lot and want to share it in a way that is very practical so that anyone, anywhere can benefit from it and succeed in the small business realm, all to the glory of God." I fully support the idea that it is much better to "teach people to fish rather than give them a fish". This book's purpose is to teach people to develop their own support, in their own culture and in their own language. The contents of this book are aimed primarily with small business owners in mind.

The Essential Elements of starting a business of any kind, anywhere.

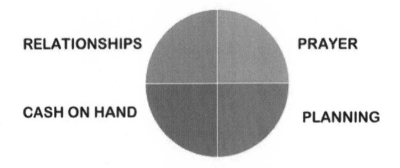

RELATIONSHIPS   PRAYER

CASH ON HAND   PLANNING

Finally, this book has been set up as a PowerPoint presentation, which can take two to three days of classroom time, including workshops, small group activities and presentations by the students. The elements of this book have been shared with audiences in Africa, Europe, Asia, North America and South America. In each place, the presentation is modified to fit the local culture so that people can use the information more readily to their own benefit. After more than 20 presentations during a 7-year period, it has proven to be of great benefit and adaptable to each culture. However, there is one key learning that has emerged from these many presentations. Lecturers normally give the "talk" and go home. An essential part is still missing. Many of the people who hear the lecture have real issues and questions about business that they want to discuss. But often their question or concern is not for public forum. There is a large demand for someone to counsel them "after" the talk. Therefore, the speaker needs to work with a local team. The local team members should take the responsibility to discuss individual questions, and be trained to use the principles outlined in this book. For the lecturer, this has proven to be the most

14

rewarding outcome of the training outlined herein. It changes people's lives! Better stated: "God changes people's lives."

Throughout this book, there are many references to the Bible and a relationship with the Lord. A key objective of the book is to teach people how to build a "Kingdom Business", no matter what culture they are in. What should a Kingdom Business look like? This is summarized below:

- A kingdom business is well managed and not in chaos (I Corinthians 14:40)
- It is socially responsible in the community (Mark 12:17, Romans 13:1-10)
- It produces income as an example of helping the local economy (Acts 18:1-4)
- It brings glory to God (I Corinthians 10:31-33)
- It promotes the growth of local churches
- It focuses on the unevangelized
- It pays all debts quickly and does not take advantage of people (Proverbs 22:7)
- It builds and sustains a good reputation for honesty and integrity in the community in which it resides.

Crossing the cultural divide can be daunting. Throughout this book there will be many examples of considerations needed when teaching before a non-North American audience. By way of introduction, here is but one such example taken from Sub-Saharan Africa.

Having given this course in Cote d'Ivoire several times, I wish to write some introductory words which reflect my experience there. The response was excellent, and this edition of the book reflects the key learnings. The purpose of the course in Africa was to equip local people to work within their native environment in a way that sets a Godly example for all to see in every community.

Below, I have listed some observations about the people of sub-Saharan Africa which should be kept in mind by teachers of this course or readers of this book. Much of the following has world-wide application.

People who live in small towns and villages need to be given a vision of what is possible for them. For the most part, someone born in a small town or city tends to look towards moving out of their town to a larger city where they can seek some work opportunities. The mayors of small towns would prefer to see their people remain there and build up the prosperity of the town, rather than move away. These leaders want to create jobs. This book helps with that objective.

People need to see that just 'getting by' is not good enough. With proper help and training, they can excel at something where they live. This book is aimed at helping them do better than they ever thought possible.

There are some barriers in the societies in Africa which seem to stifle good planning. The ability to plan ahead is a basic business need. This course/book addresses that need and trains people how to plan in the formation of their businesses and how to sustain them.

There is a need to build self-motivation within many people. The prevailing belief is that something needs to be given to them first before they can start. This course gives them training, nothing else. This course/book will motivate many of them to be self-starters and put their minds to work on new, creative ideas.

Much that could be done in Africa is not being done because people simply are not informed about what is going on outside their own culture. This course encourages people to get informed. Association with people from the outside who can share their experiences and ideas is badly needed. This course has many illustrations using actual examples of what others have done to create and sustain businesses.

This course is open to all who desire to improve their businesses, regardless of religion, gender, language or nationality.

Time has a different value in Africa than it does in Europe or North America. Those who wish to train African people in business practices, must take into account what is meant in the west by the expression "time is money". This isn't so in Africa. For a variety of reasons, people will be late for appointments and think nothing of it. People may be late in meeting business obligations too, and think nothing of that. Being 'late' isn't 'bad business' or improper behavior in sub-Saharan Africa. Nor is it bad behavior in Latin America. People who come late to meetings always seem to blame the traffic, but never apologize for failing to take that "traffic" into consideration when planning to come to the meeting. They never have a "cushion" built in. They know the traffic is awful, so plan for it!

African cultures place high value on age. In some rural settings, a younger member of a business organization may have difficulty in putting forth his or her 'good idea' if an older member of the organization says that it can't be done.

In many western cultures, people respect numbers and calculations. This is perhaps done to a fault in the western cultures, without knowing much about the people they are working with. In sub-Saharan Africa, people are generally not trained to 'calculate' but place their trust in word of mouth, handshakes and personal relationships. This course teaches students the importance of calculations. In small groups, they will be encouraged to practice simple yet very important calculations.

Sub-Saharan Africa is a group of 'reciprocity-based' cultures. If you (or your business) has some money, and someone else needs it and asks for it, it is common to give to that person in need. In this way, you as the business owner accumulate a circle of others who 'owe you a favor'. It is really hard to break that pattern and hence, the business is often lacking in money because it was simply given away! Have fun with that one!

In many parts of the world, poor planning and inefficiency is a problem. Here is just one example:

A certain city maintained a fleet of city buses, 30 in all. They circulated around the city on their prescribed routes each day. If just one of the buses had a flat tire, there was a big problem. Among the 30 buses, there was only one spare tire, and it was on one of the buses. But that bus carried no tire jack. That was on another bus. If you were unfortunate enough to have a flat tire, the wait for both of the buses which had the spare equipment might be quite long!

Dealing with inefficiency can be maddening to someone seeking to start and sustain a business.

The "government", or lack of it, can be a major obstacle to establishing a business in most parts of the world today. Being buffaloed and bamboozled by a blizzard of bungling bureaucracy can discourage the most stout-hearted entrepreneur! One has to contend with a large number of meaningless "approvals" before work can begin. In one country in which I worked; 26 such approvals were required given by individuals who had these largely "invented jobs" made up for them by friends in local, state and national government.

Taxes are "variable" in so many parts of the world. It is very common for a company to keep two sets of books; one to show to the government for tax basis, and the other to keep a more accurate record of what the business is really earning. Corruption is the common way to convince the tax collector to accept the lower record of earnings. Pay them off! The problem of corruption is rampant and chapter 10 deals with it in more detail. Many companies try to avoid paying taxes until they are caught and fined.

In many parts of this world, there is a "Severe Poverty Mindset". Their needs overwhelm all else that they might do. "You come here to teach me about business!" What that really means is that they want you to give them everything they need and after doing that, allow them to mismanage it in any way they want to. You will find examples of people in this book who think out of that box, and plan well even though they live in impoverished areas. Be encouraged by that!

- "It's kind of fun to do the impossible" Walt Disney
- "Culture eats strategy for breakfast!" Peter Drucker

Working in any cultural climate is daunting at the least, and seemingly impossible at the worst, but never forget….

"With man, it is impossible, but with God all things are possible." Matthew 19:26b.

ACKNOWLEDGEMENTS

I would like to given special acknowledgement and thanks to my wife, Suzanne, who put up with my absence while I spent hours writing this book.

I would also like to give thanks to the Lord who inspired me to write these pages and who furnished me with so many personal examples that I can share. His inspiration was felt throughout the writing.

Many friends contributed ideas for this book as well, and for them, I am grateful. I especially value the help and suggestions of Glenn Gerhard, an entrepreneur and owner of the Silk City Coffee in Manchester, CT whose advice and personal experiences were shared and much appreciated. Another is my friend Gene Ontjes, owner of two Chic-Fil-A's in the Philadelphia area. A third person who contributed to my aims for this book is Tim Glavin, owner of a limo business In Wilmington, DE. All of these friends and many conversations and suggestions are deeply appreciated.

I am so grateful for the 37 years that I worked for the DuPont Company, and from which the knowhow about justifying business proposals was learned. My profession was the crucible that God provided to give me priceless experience.

The publication of this book was completed on Amazon Kindle Direct Publishing by Charlie Liebert.
charlie@sixdaycreation.com

I wish you great success as you develop your businesses!! Do it for the Lord!

Chapter 1 One Page Business Plan

Subject:	One Page Business Plan
Lesson Objectives:	To prepare you to think about what will be required of you when you start on your business venture.
	To provide a list of important considerations which will be reviewed from time to time after the business is started
	To provide some clarity of vision and to prompt you to think about how you can execute that vision or plan.
	To fix in your mind and heart what a kingdom business looks like.
Book Recommended	Several one-page business plan forms are available on the internet

Introduction

This exercise is designed to help you think about your business plan, which will be covered in much more detail in Chapter 5. It will cover some of the most important questions which you will face when going before a board of directors, an advisory board, or a lending institution from which you may want to borrow capital. See how well you can answer these questions.

Elements of a One Page Business Plan

What am I building? What is my intention for the future? Where am I now, and where do I want to be in 5 or 10 years? How does this fit in with God's plan for my life? Ref Ephesians 2:10.

Why am I building this? What are my motivations?

How will I build it? Do I have capital of my own, or must I borrow it?

What is the work to be done, as outlined by certain 'milestones'? When do I expect the work to start and finish? What insures that this timeline is do-able?

What are the metrics by which progress and success will be measured?

How do I define what a "Kingdom Business" means, as it pertains to the business I am proposing? How do I intend to create an environment which glorifies God in my business?

You are a trustee of God's business. What is the written agreement between you and God as you carry out His business? Ref: Matthew 25:14-30 and Luke 19:12-28. What does God want you to know about carrying out business for Him? How do you intend to stay accountable to God? Who will be on your board of directors for accountability? Write answers to these questions in the space below.

You will find an example of a one-page business plan on the next page. This example is based on an idea that would be given to a potential investor. At this point, you are not asking for a capital investment loan, but simply a show of interest. The interest shown demonstrates that once your plan is better developed, you can return and make a serious request for investment capital and other forms of support. Based on what you have at that point means you may or may not get your request. This example is written for a business proposed in Sao Paulo, Brazil, but it could be anywhere. Is anything missing?

Business Plan Example – The Bridge School

TITLE: THE BRIDGE SCHOOL

I propose to begin a school for students who need practical experience after graduating from a university. This school, named "The Bridge School", will add skills to the students which will help them get a job, and helps them gain a more solid idea of what career they wish to pursue. These skills include translation abilities, public speaking, debating, interviewing a prospective employer, team work and writing proficiencies in a way that helps them become more productive members of Brazil's society. This school is designed to be a one-year program.

This school will train about 250 students per year. Each student will pay a tuition fee which will make the school a break-even profit or perhaps a slightly positive cash flow from year to year. The first school will begin in Sao Paulo, but in the future, more schools like this one are envisioned for this city and other cities in Brazil.

The lectures will be given by people who have gained expertise in each field and who will come to teach voluntarily. Courses such as these will be offered:

- Entrepreneurship: how to begin and sustain a business of any size
- Resume preparation and interviewing prospective employers
- Talking before audiences either in person or using video technology
- Submitting ideas to a company and defending them effectively
- English proficiency in speaking, writing and reading, and translating before an audience
- Building and maintaining good health habits
- Development of excellent computer skills for use in any workplace

The school will advertise through social media, local publications and personal references. Initially, we expect to have 200 students in our rented facility, with growth to 250 before seeking to locate a second site. Each student will receive a certificate of accomplishment.

We expect that the annual budget for this school will be 600.000 reais and that the annual income will be the same, derived mostly from student tuition. There will be no capital investment. A staff of about 15 will be needed to manage this enterprise.

Finally, we anticipate that a second school will begin in another part of Sao Paulo, using the same model, and by the 20th year of operation, we look forward to having 5 such schools in the country. We wish to help our students achieve their professional dreams.

Note what is included in the one-page business plan, and what is not included. At this point, it is simply an expression of an idea. There is no "hard data", no fact checking, no basis in research. None of the numbers are supported by solid information. There is no marketing study which would support that there is even interest in the city for such a school. There is no research to show if there are already other such schools in the region. Has such a thing been tried before and failed? How is this idea better than the apprenticeship programs of Europe, or co-op schools in Canada and the USA, such as Purdue University? It is a "gleam in your eye" at this point. Can you take this idea and get busy people to read the one page, and show interest? If you manage to find interest, the next step is to do all the hard work of gathering information, and then bring it back for serious review, many questions and a capital request.

By doing a one-page business plan, you have brought your idea into some focus, so that it can be explained to others (and yourself). That is a very necessary first step.

This should be done with a small team of knowledgeable people at your side. There is wisdom in many counselors (ref. Proverbs 11:14, 15:22 and 24:6). Such a plan should not be developed alone.

A Business Model Canvas

Another step beyond the "One Page Business Plan" is to develop the well-known "Business Model Canvas". It is a grid diagram, readily found on the internet in many forms, which lists the key pieces of information needed when considering a business. The first things listed are:

- State the business idea: Training school to prepare students for the workplace
- State the business model: For profit, privately owned enterprise
- Products and services: Training classes, internships, certificate of achievement

The grid below lists columns of information including:

- Partners: universities, high schools, employers, volunteer teachers, government agencies
- Activities: garner support from schools, and companies who might take an intern for a certain length of time. What is a fair price for students to pay, etc?
- Value offered: Define what value the students will receive, and what makes this school different from others who may be in the region.
- Customer relations: How can we recruit students? How modern must our technology be? Who are "really" our customers, the students or the companies who employ them once they graduate?
- Market segment: What market rate of growth can we expect? How much beyond our offering are we willing to go? Is this a mass market, or a niche market? How many paying customers can we expect?

This canvas contains no answers. It simply lists the questions which are important to help guide you as you press on. It is useful to connect some of the entries in a logical order of what must happen before something else can happen, similar to a Gantt chart.

There is no mention of any plan to honor God in the One Page Business Plan example or in the business model canvas. There should be. What kind of spiritual impact do you expect this plan to have on your community?

Does the title of the One Page Business Plan or the Canvas Model seem compelling? Does the title and the opening line rivet your attention in a way that says to you or those you are trying to interest "Read On!!" If they are not compelling, then rethink what you are saying in your title and opening line.

It is important to emphasize that neither the One Page Business Plan, or the Business Model Canvas, is a substitute for a full, well-done business plan. The full business plan will be explained in more detail in Chapter 5. Many people make the mistake of thinking they are now done, having gone just this far. This is not so; instead, the "real" work will now begin

Chapter 2 Creativity & Ingenuity

Subject:	Creating something from nothing
Lesson Objectives:	Where do you begin to create your business?
	Understand the difference between creating and copying
	How to gather and evaluate different ideas
Special Supplies	Chart paper, masking tape and several markers
Books recommended	"The Lean Startup", Eric Ries

Introduction

No business can succeed for long without clarity of vision. If you cannot articulate what you want to do, no one else can do it for you. A man told me once that he wanted to "get into manufacturing", but had no idea what he wanted to manufacture. It took many discussions before something clear was developed. In the next module, we will do a "Feasibility Study", but first we need to write a long list of potential business ideas for consideration. We need to be imaginative, creative and very honest with ourselves. We need to know ourselves well. We need the honest input from others who know us well.

Where can we begin?

A good place to begin is by reading examples from the Bible, which tells us to pray and to give our business to God. Consider Matthew 6:26 in which God takes care of the birds. He gives them good eyes, strong wings, energy and good instincts. But does He build the nests for them? No. Does He go and find the insects to provide food for their families and drop it into the nests while they wait? No. God expects them to work hard and provide for themselves, and to use their natural abilities. So we must use our minds to think of ways to create our own opportunities.

A list of ideas which you might consider may look like this:

- Raising chickens and selling the eggs
- Selling clothing that you either make, or buy for resale
- Providing a taxi service with either a motorbike or a car
- Making and selling baskets
- Lending money
- Internet café
- Cell phone service (new and used)
- Buying plastic scrap from factories and reselling it
- Coffee shop and cybercafé combination
- Clothing repair shop
- Haircuts
- Restaurant
- Prepare taxes for other businesses
- Build roads in places where roads are in bad condition
- Use urine to make light for homes (what?? really??)
- Bicycle, motorbike or car repair shop
- Refining palm oil and selling it
- Day care for small children
- Day care center for the elderly
- Medical clinic to treat common ailments
- Fruit and vegetable market
- Flower shop
- Language lessons
- Laundry services and clothing repair
- Typing documents for people
- Making copies of documents for people
- Selling fuel for cars and motorbikes
- Making jewelry

- Selling solar panels or solar cookers
- Making furniture
- Making doors using local lumber
- Dental care
- Coffee bean collecting, drying, grinding, bagging, shipping
- Learning another language well enough to offer translation services to visitors, lecturers, writers, etc.

Here are some examples of what some people have done to start and grow their businesses, some successfully and others not.

Chicha morada is a very popular drink in Peru. It is made from purple corn. A man has a cornfield, and he hires ladies to press the corn into corn juice, from which chicha morada is made. He does not own a store, but instead, he has his business in a large church in his city. He loves God and gives 15% of the profits from his business to Him. The remaining profits are used to buy more corn fields and plant more corn. As he does this, his business grows. He sells the chicha morada by having a small sign outside the church during the weekdays.

One day, a man walked in and asked for a job. The owner was able to see that this man would be a good salesman. So he bought the man a nice suit and tie, and hired him to sit at a table, on the sidewalk, and offer free samples of his drink to people who passed by. The man did prove to be a good salesman, and he convinced many new people to become customers. The business more than doubled! Each time the profits were counted, 15% went to the Lord's work, and the rest was used to buy new fields and plant more corn.

He now has several such operations in that city! He decided then to give his salesman not only a salary, but 5% of the profits as well. Since that time, his total sales have greatly increased!

Such good treatment of his salesman, encouraged that man to come to the owner with an idea: instead of selling one bottle of chicha morada at a time for $1, wrap two of them together and sell those for $1.75. You can even buy a "party pack" of 6 bottles for $5!

As a result, the total sales have increased to double what they were before!

Where do you see wisdom, creativity and ingenuity in this true story?

1. He did not go deeply into debt at the beginning
2. He was determined that God owned his business
3. Giving customers good value and treating them honestly has brought him a good reputation and even more customers.
4. He started small and worked up
5. He had a bigger vision than just one store
6. He had good insight about who to hire and treated the man well
7. He saw that the status quo way of doing business could be made better.
8. He recognized a common need and was able to fill that need.
9. He listened to the suggestions of his employee.
10. He held some profits in reserve, so when the time was right, he could invest it in more fields for growing purple corn.
11. The salesman was honest with the owner and did not save some of the profit for himself, knowing that he was trusted and well paid.
12. He kept cash inside his business by properly balancing his accounts payables and his accounts receivables.

Where could he have gotten into trouble? He would be greatly at risk…..

- If he has one health complaint from a customer who gets sick from chicha morada.
- If he cheats his customers

- If mistreats his employees
- If he hires other employees who are dishonest and steal from the owner
- If he handles his employees so poorly that there is high turnover and he is constantly having to train new people.

Another example:

Akinori Ito lives in Japan, and values the cleanliness of the country like most of his countrymen. Plastic trash, however, is a growing problem, and many people simply throw plastic containers, films, etc away. Since these materials are made from petroleum, they will never decompose, but will remain a pollutant on the land and streets. If they are simply burned, they will pollute the air with carbon dioxide. Ito-san converted a high-pressure pot usually used for cooking, into a vessel for heating plastic trash to 400 C and reducing it back to petroleum. He uses a bucket of water to cool down and condense the gases from the plastic, and makes 'petroleum' again, which can be used for heating, fuel for cars, and many other high value uses. He takes his equipment to groups of school children also, and tries to inspire them to think about ways to do it even better. Ito-san hopes that he can sell one set of his equipment to every home and business, and then collect the 'petroleum' that comes from it and sell it to large companies for a profit.

Where do you see creativity and ingenuity in this true story?

- He did not go deeply into debt to develop his business, but used common equipment that can be bought in a store. Higher investment may come later if he decides to scale up.
- He recognized a big problem with pollution and he was troubled by it
- He worked hard, with many failures, before he succeeded.
- He took some risks; the gases which come from the 'cooker' are flammable!

- He is happy to share his idea with school children and many others.

Another example:

Four high school girls (ages 14-15) in Lagos, Nigeria listened to their chemistry teacher. They lived outside the city, where electricity was either non-existent, or unreliable. Homes in the villages often do not have electricity at all. Solar panels and wind turbines are far too expensive for most people. As they listened in class to a discussion about electrolytic cells, they had an idea. Pure water conducts no electricity, but salty water does! In every home, there is a supply of urine, so why not use it? They devised an electrolytic cell to generate current to power several light bulbs, and also purify the water so it could be used for washing. They controlled the odor using bicarbonate of soda, and some borax to purify the water. Their electrolytic cell generates 6 hours of power for several light bulbs, per liter of urine! The girls hope to go into business selling their systems, which don't take up much space, to many homes and businesses who can't rely on the local electrical grid. The supply of raw material is assured and always cheap!

Where do you see creativity and ingenuity in this true story?

- The girls paid attention in class, and learned about a principle they could use.
- The girls saw a problem that needed to be solved
- The girls saw an abundant, "worthless" raw material which was not being used. This raw material is free!
- The girls worked hard together as a team to combine the principle they learned with the need they saw and used the raw materials at hand.
- They were willing to give up other activities enjoyed by people their age for a higher value activity with long term benefits.

One of the most attention-grabbing efforts today, at least in North America and Europe, is to either recycle plastics or replace the use of plastics with something more biodegradable. One biodegradable product that has been developed, is the use of potatoes for dinner ware and other instruments (knives, forks, etc).

Growing Potatoes to make "plastic"

All compostable items; no pollution!

Tater Ware

While these items made from polyethylene will never degrade, the same produced from Grade B potatoes will compost back into the ground after about one year. Grade A potatoes are those with no flaws, and are sold in the market. Grade B potatoes are those which have been damaged and cannot be sold. Any variety of potato will do. They are practically given away, and are boiled down into a wet paste. Then they are dried to remove the 50% water they contain, and the resultant fibrous material is mixed with stiffeners to make it moldable. The high fiber content of potatoes helps to make the dinnerware strong enough to be used for serving food, washed and reused a few times, before discarding. Is this a feasible idea? See the next chapter 3, about feasibility. Developed when the price of petroleum, and therefore the price of polyethylene, was high, these seemed like a good idea. Technically, they work. Financially, it is very hard to compete with cheaper oil. Clever idea, however!

34

How to be creative

Being creative is almost essential to succeeding in business. Creativity is mostly an in-born gift from God, whether creative people acknowledge Him or not. If the entrepreneur is not especially creative, then they need to encourage an atmosphere of creativity within the workforce around them. Creativity is essential because:

- It is often the basis of a good business idea
- It provides new business beyond the ones you currently have
- It allows for better solutions and often better profit margins

Creativity requires a company culture that respects effort and failure. If you are not gifted with creativity, you will need some people who work for you who are creative. Creativity comes from special moments, when you see something in your mind that "puts the pieces together and it starts to make sense". Notable people who have demonstrated creativity and succeeded very well include:

Henry Ford…did not build the first car or invent the car, but had the idea that everyone should be able to afford one. He created the idea of the assembly line for production, based on what he saw one day watching sausages being made in a meat factory. By making them on an assembly line, he could make them cheaper and affordable to the average working man.

Thomas Edison….knew that a long-burning light bulb should be possible and built one experimental model after the other, trying more than 10,000 times, until he found a material (tungsten) that would work. He once said "I know 10,000 ways in which a light bulb will not work!" Determined? Yes! Work hard? Yes! Give up? Never! Edison holds 1093 U.S. patents!

J D Rockefeller saw the advantages of petroleum before others did, and knew that whale oil could not last forever. He went deeply in debt to invest in finding oil, failing many times, before he finally made it work. Once he demonstrated how to make kerosene from petroleum, the whale oil business was finished almost overnight, and petroleum oil became one of the most valuable commodities on the planet.

Emma, the Girl Scout who sold thousands of cookies to car dealers for a 4-way win.

My granddaughter, Emma, is a Girl Scout, and sells Girl Scout cookies every year with the rest of her troop. The traditional way to sell them is to ask all of your relatives to buy them. Typically, a girl scout might sell 30 boxes a year. Emma got an idea to make up a presentation on her laptop, advertising all the different flavors of cookies. She took her laptop to automobile dealers in her area. She dressed up in her scout uniform, and approached many general managers of dealerships. She suggested to them that if they would buy a whole carton of 100 boxes each, and give a free box to every car customer who came in and test drove a new car, he could write it off as a business expense on his taxes and attract more customers. It worked! She sells 2000-3000 boxes each year! Creative? Yes! Shy to approach new people with her ideas? No!

This true story is not about cookies. The story is about how to see potential in something small and simple. Emma focused on devising a way in which everyone could become a 'winner'.

There were no losers. There were four winners!

1. The Girl Scout organization had more income
2. Emma was given credit and an award
3. The car dealer gained popularity with his customers, and he was able to write off the cost of the cookies on his income taxes as a business expense
4. The customer was given a test drive in a new car and a free box of cookies

Thin Mints   Caramel deLites®   Peanut Butter Patties®   Peanut Butter Sandwiches®

Shortbread   Thanks-A-Lot™   Lemonades™   Shout Outs!™

What can you do with your business by thinking in a similar way?

Create a culture of creativity

Here are some ways to foster creativity within your business, no matter how large or small it may be.

Search out new experiences and perspectives

Learn the art of asking many questions that are not open ended, answerable by "yes" or "no". Write down the answers and take them seriously. Learn to ask "powerful questions", to be addressed in more detail in chapter 6. Learn to engage in "fierce conversations" that get decisions and motivate people into action to try new things.

Respect other people and their ideas, no matter who they are. I always talked with those who operated and maintained the equipment and learned so much when trying to solve problems in the factory in which I worked.

Don't mind it if some people think you are crazy or annoying.

Always give credit to those who gave you the idea. Don't pretend that it was your idea alone.

Challenge yourself by setting personal goals to brainstorm and develop new ideas

Go away and think for certain periods of time. Allow yourself to invent new ideas which would help the business and devise ways to try them without risking the business.

Seek and build relationships with people who are different than you are

They help you and you help them

"Anything is possible, if you don't care who gets the credit" (Ronald Reagan).

Learn to enjoy asking questions of everybody. You're not "interrogating them", you are including them.

Create a culture which respects effort and failure

There are some jobs in which 'creativity' may not be welcomed. For example, a nurse on the hospital floor should not try to be too creative when treating a patient, nor should a teller at a bank try to create new ways of handling money, without being very careful. But a nurse working in a poor village with no hospital and few resources must be creative! An operator working in a nuclear power plant should not try to be "creative" unless boundaries are well understood and many people are involved in "trying something new".

There are jobs which depend on being creative. Research, for example, depends on creativity. So does success in business! Entrepreneurs should think "out of the box" (like Emma the Girl Scout did)

In some cultures, failure is looked upon with shame. Properly handled, this should not be the case. One person's failure can save repeating that same costly mistake by another person. Look upon every honest effort as having value.

Remember that creativity usually costs money. There aren't many free experiments. That money may be yours, in which you have more freedom to be creative, or it may be someone else's, and you are more restricted in just how creative you can be. Too much 'unsuccessful creativity' might cost you your job! When you have a creative idea, think carefully about what the costs will be. Will you create yourself out of a job?

In the Bible, in Matthew 25:14-30, the master gave 10 talents (a unit of currency) to one man, 5 to another, and 1 to a third man. They were to create ways to protect it and bring it back with interest when the master returned. The first two did that. The last servant, with one talent, buried it in the ground. Why did he do that? He was afraid of failure, of being compared with others. The master condemned him. He lost the one talent he had and it was given to one of the others who had demonstrated better stewardship. Point: Invest your skills, resources and creativity! Don't bury it and have nothing to show for it, and then make excuses why progress was not made!

Reward creativity in a way that encourages it. It isn't always money.

I was greatly encouraged when my company gave me a simple directive to go establish businesses which made a profit in a reasonable period of time. There were few controls; mainly trust. I thrived in an environment in which I was given a chance to be creative, and it worked very well. My rewards were mostly recognition and the chances to do the same again and again. Some companies give "seed money" to employees whom they believe can put it to good, creative use. (More discussion on that experience in Chapter 3)

Create a culture of continuous improvement

W. Edwards Deming had ideas for improving the quality of automobiles produced in the USA, and his ideas were turned down by all of the major manufacturers. He decided to take his ideas to post-war Japan, and there he found an enthusiastic audience. The Japanese loved his ideas for examining what could have been done better. Each day, the whole team, from top management to the average worker, would get together to discuss what small aspect of their autos could be improved upon. They examined each mistake that was made the day before and resolved it. This was done without reprimanding any one person. As a result, the reputation they had for being sub-standard quality became one of superior quality, and car sales went up significantly! They created a 'culture of continuous improvement'.

Deming also gave an example of being in the 'wrong business'. For years, autos used carburetors as a means of mixing the fuel with air and burning it to provide power for the engine. Entire factories were built to make carburetors and engineers became the best in their field at designing them. Then, one day, the fuel injector was introduced, and almost overnight, the carburetor was no longer needed. Those people should have been thinking about what business they were really in! They should not have been in the "carburetor business" but in the "automobile combustion engine" business, and thinking how to make themselves obsolete....before someone else did! You must keep pace with changing times. Creating a 'culture of continuous improvement' means to look beyond the task of the day and into the future to anticipate what changes may take place which will affect your business. How would you create such a culture in your business?

To summarize, it can be said that

- **Creativity is needed to find clever ways to solve problems**
- **Creativity is seeing opportunities which 'might' make a good business, and then exploring them.**
- **Creativity needs to be rewarded and honored, no matter who puts forth the idea.**
- **Creativity can get a company into trouble if the idea is not thoroughly explored.**

Sometimes, creativity can lead to 'disruptive technology', explained well by Dr. Clayton Christensen. This phenomenon happens when a new technology completely replaces an older one making it forever obsolete. For example, horse drawn vehicles were not really replaced by the invention of the automobile because all autos were made one at a time and were therefore only affordable by the wealthy few. But, when Henry Ford came up with the assembly line idea, and costs for autos fell drastically and everyone could afford one, then the need for horse drawn vehicles practically vanished. The disruptive technology was the idea of the assembly line! By 1910, it was very unwise to start a horse drawn vehicle manufacturing business. Time to get into automobiles! When you are considering a business, you must plan for someone to disrupt it at some time in the future and putting you out of business!

- Did the television put the radio out of business?
- Did the CD put the cassette tape out of business?
- Why are internet cafes going out of business?
- Why are shopping malls struggling to stay in business? Some of them are ghost towns!
- Perhaps you should think about how you might "disrupt" what you are doing, and put yourself out of business!

Final advice about creativity

Talk with many people, take many notes, think carefully and give credit where credit is due. Pray earnestly over each decision, asking the Holy Spirit to guide your thoughts. Is now the time, or not? Then proceed. Chapters on feasibility, developing a sales & marketing plan, a hiring plan, a business plan, and an executive summary come next!

Exercises

A. Break up into smaller groups of 4 or 5. I am "giving you" these things to work with and I want you to come with a creative way to use them. You have 30 minutes.

Each group will get a "basket" with these items in it:

1. 5 mangoes
2. Some plastic trash (empty bottles, plastic bags)
3. Pieces of wood
4. 15 bananas
5. 4 liters of milk in glass bottles
6. 5 loaves of bread

You do have access to water as much as you need. You also have access to any tools (knives, hammers, etc.) that you may need. At the end of your creative use of these materials, tell the rest of the group what you have done, and what tools you needed to make it.

B. Coming together as a large group, let's discuss the following problem and try to come up with some creative solutions. We will create a "wall of ideas" by writing ideas on paper and posting them on the wall. Any idea is valuable. There are no 'bad' ideas at this point. Then after 30 minutes, we will agree on a solution and list the positives and negatives of that solution. Here is the problem:

Roads and highways in this country are not in good condition. They have holes and this prevents good traffic flow and damages vehicles. The city streets are also littered with trash made up of plastic, paper and many other forms. How can the two be used together, to solve two problems at the same time, economically, safely and in a way that creates jobs for people who have no work?

Your assignment is to propose several solutions to this situation, then agree as a team which is the best solution and list the positives and negatives.

Also, propose who you might use as a resource to make sure that you have the best chance of success. Give me your proposed 'path forward' for the plan.

Words of Wisdom

Before we move on to the next chapter, here are some important things to keep in mind when selecting possible business ventures:

Follow the money. Read the news, what is happening in your city or country, talk with people, become informed! Keep aware of trends which are happening. For example, in the USA, the population is getting older. Baby boomers are retiring, and they have disposable income. What do such people do with the money they have worked hard for all of their lives? They go to restaurants, buy second homes, take vacation trips, need health care and move into retirement communities. What does that suggest where the money is flowing? Breaking it down a little further, there are three groups of people:

- Those who retire with no savings
- Those who retire but have a big debt and just enough for necessities
- Those who retire and have money for discretionary spending
- Which group will your business serve?
- In order to serve that group, where must you be located?

Follow The Money

This illustration of the oil field describes how to "follow the money". Note on that diagram how some people are employed directly by the oil well unit. There are others who don't work directly on the oil rigs, but who need supplies and transport of all kinds.

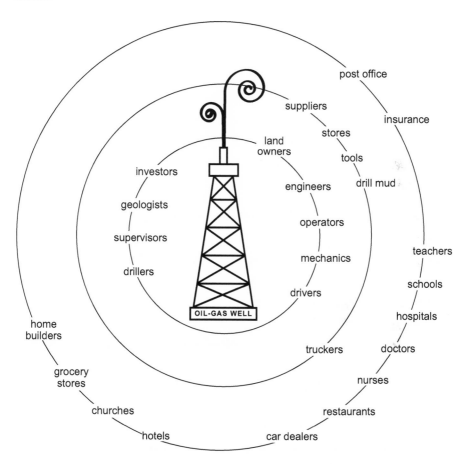

All of those need other services that meet the needs of the families of those who work on the oil rigs, such as grocery stores, hospitals, schools, law offices, auto repair, law enforcement, etc. This is an example of how money flows in a certain direction. When the money is flowing, it is good to "catch that wave" and be part of it. But we all know that the oil industry rises and falls with the price of oil, and when times get rough, those markets drift away to "greener pastures". In 2014 when oil reached $140/barrel, this was exciting. But then it fell to $40/barrel two years later. What then?

Know when to get in, and when to get out.

American singer Kenny Rogers popularized these words in his song "The Gambler".

"You've got to know when to hold 'em, know when to fold 'em; know when to walk away and know when to run".

This wisdom is key to many of the businesses which have sustained or failed. Many entrepreneurs delay getting in, or getting out, and lose most of their gains or lose opportunities.

Would anyone really invest in a manufacturing plant to make cassettes? Perhaps 20 years ago it would have been a good idea, but technology has eclipsed cassettes by now. Even internet cafes, very popular some 20 years ago, are past their prime. Everyone has their own laptops and smart phones now. No need to go to an internet café. Sewing machines have been around for over 100 years, and what is happening to them? Really, nothing! In many parts of the world, in both well developed and under-developed ones, the sewing machine is an essential part of many families. A man in Huancayo, Peru has a sewing machine repair business in his home and is doing very well. The point is to keep aware of where the markets are, and are not. Keep aware of technologies which are being rapidly replaced and those which cannot be. How many nail salons can a town really support? If one were to go into that business, what would you offer which is different or unique that might draw people to your salon instead of the one just up the street? More discussion of this critical topic is found in chapter 4. Know when to get in, when not to get in, and when to get out!

Learn Where The Money Is Flowing And Follow It

Meet a need. Where in a chain of activities will you choose to place yourself? Are you going to go into business by…

- Manufacturing something?
- Building the facilities to manufacture something?
- Advertising something?
- Selling something?
- Transporting something?
- Inventing something?
- Distributing something?
- Servicing something?
- Researching something to make it better?
- Or will you choose to do some or all of these together?

Each choice has major implications about how much capital you need, how much expertise you need, and how big your organization must be.

Learn from History

Why repeat the mistakes of others? Know what happened and learn from them. Ask questions and read reports! Become very informed. An astute gentleman said these words: "those who ignore history and the failures of the past, are condemned to repeat them." Sir Winston Churchill

Much more will be said about the reasons why so many businesses fail, in chapter 8.

God must guide your thoughts and your actions

If you have agreed to allow God to be your senior partner in your business, then in what creative ways can you show that to those who deal with you? How can you have a spiritual impact on your community? A couple of examples will suffice for now:

MyPillow, Inc, is a firm in Minnesota which manufactures pillows and other bedding materials. This company employed about 1600 people in 2019, up from 5 in 2009. The inventor of the pillow design and the owner of the business is Mike Lindell. His testimony is very much in the news as a Christian entrepreneur who came from a troubled background. He lived on the street, lost his family and home, and was addicted to crack cocaine. One day, he gave his heart and his business to Christ and made Him in charge of his life. His children returned to him as young adults and they worked together in efforts to invent a better pillow. Today he is very vocal about his love for Christ to his employees and to the public. Of the 1600 employees, about 1/3 of them are former drug addicts and prisoners. He honors God in many clear ways, leaving no doubt who really owns his business.

It is important to note that Mr. Lindell is in the bedding business, not the pillow business. He produces not only pillows, but sheets, mattress toppers, comforters, and even sleep wear for pets. He is not only an expert on pillows, but on how to get a good night's sleep! He must have read from W. Edwards Deming's writings. Would it be wise for him to go into the tractor business or open a restaurant? Would it be wise for him to start manufacturing pharmaceuticals to help people sleep? Not advisable! That would be outside his area of expertise. There is wisdom in defining who you are and developing the business in a way that lets you change with the times and not stagnate or get left behind.

Optimum Performance Chiropractic is a firm in Delaware owned by Dr. Mike Francis. His firm has about 12 employees and offers many varieties of treatments for people in pain or who simply need "readjustment". Many years ago, Dr. Mike gave his heart and his business to God, and this is evidenced in the way that the office appears, with verses of Scripture in each office and music being played. The evidence is subtle, but clear. Little doubt that Dr.

Mike's business is owned by God. His mission statement is on the office wall:

PRAY OFTEN   WORK HARD   TRUST GOD

Again, we find a business which is not simply in the classic "chiropractic" business, but is in the skeletal wellness business, offering a range of cryogenic treatments and exercises aimed at lowering pain levels in bones, joints and muscles. Everything he offers is well within his area of expertise.

Discussion questions

A. How do you apply this instruction from Christ? (see chapters 3 and 4). "What man will build a tower without first sitting down and counting the cost?" Luke 14:28-33

B. What is wisdom and where does it come from? James 1:5 "If any of you lacks wisdom, let him ask it from God, who gives to all men liberally, and it shall be given to him."

C. What is integrity? In Genesis 39 Joseph refused to fall into temptation, and paid a high price for keeping his integrity. But in the end, he was very well rewarded and used by God.

D. What is the difference between creating work of your own, and copying someone else's work, claiming that it is yours? Why is the difference important? Perhaps the "Golden Rule" applies? "Do to others as you would have them do to you."

E. What business are you doing now, and how can you better define it? What ideas does this give you for changing your business?

Given the business you have right now, how could it be replaced in the future and put you out of business? What can you do about that?

Creativity can have many forms. In my case, I spent my life working for a large corporation which had many departments which often didn't speak to each other. Each existed in their own kingdom, or "silo". One was making synthetic fiber and experiencing the normal manufacturing losses of 10%. This amounted to a very large volume of material which was landfilled each year. The department I worked for used that same synthetic material but in a different form; plastic resins, not fiber. I devised a way to melt that thermoplastic fiber again, melt-filtering it and making blends of plastic useful for the molded parts industries. Another department insisted that the engineering work be done using their expertise. I insisted that I use individual machinery vendors to do that, and that I do it with standard models rather than paying a fortune for special, made to order models of equipment. This saved millions of dollars. In so doing, the vendors of equipment held the responsibility to make own equipment work, or else fix it. Once the factory was built and all of the operating instructions were written and operator training was done, the plant started up. At start up, the entire project was well under budget, on time, and safely done. The process, proven out on individual equipment at the vendor's shops, was successful except for one part. That part, a melt filter, was critical to the success of the venture. When it failed, I had a backup plan to put in a different design. That design worked well. From the first day of operation, all 45 operators and mechanics and laboratory personnel knew what to do and took pride in their jobs. That startup was 36 years ago, and the plant is still running and has been expanded several times to be the home for over 200 employees. Creativity was shown in doing things differently than the "norm", being sure of what to expect and knowing how to react if a problem occurred and creating an environment in which new ideas are rewarded. The payback on that plant's operation was about 2 years and has earned millions of dollars for the company.

Another example of business success is the Silk City Coffee, in Manchester, Connecticut. It is a coffee shop on Main Street that has been in business for about five years. The atmosphere is friendly and inviting, the service is great, and while the owners are Christians, the other employees are a mixture of Christian and non. The food offerings are not broad, but what is offered is tasty in this relaxed area which is well located, easy to find, offers easy parking and in particular, a wall board on which anybody can place personal prayer requests. The owners take that seriously and pray for people and even with people if that is requested.

Creating the right atmosphere is important anywhere in the world. Much of North Africa has a French colonial tradition. As such, coffee shops abound. In one city there are universities, but no coffee shops in the immediate area. Students want the coffee shop lifestyle, where they can meet some people their own age and do some studying. I observed that many of them will drive across this large city, taking an hour in traffic, to come to this one shop named "The Family Place".

They pass dozens of other coffee shops to do this. It is a private Christian business, in a French colonial house with three floors. A coffee shop on the ground floor, classrooms for English training on the next and physical workout space and equipment on the next. Superb coffee and American desserts (fudge brownies, cheesecake, etc) are served. Arab students love this place. One girl said to me that she comes several times a week. Why? "Because when I come, I walk in with no friends, and in two hours, I leave with 10 friends!"

The Family Place, in North Africa.

The place is irresistible! How about your business? Is it equally irresistible? And In addition, unlike other coffee shops, customers must become members and pay a membership fee!

Chapter 3 Feasibility Plan

Subject:	Feasibility Study or Plan
Lesson Objectives:	Understand what a feasibility study is and how it helps in the development of a business plan
	Understand the difference between a feasibility study and a business plan
	Participants will be able to describe each stage of a feasibility study and to prepare a written report
Books Recommended	Many Wikipedia articles are available on the internet
	"Fundamentals of Corporate Finance", Brealey, Myers, Marcus

Introduction

Perhaps the most crucial problem you will face after expressing an interest in starting a new business or capitalizing on an apparent opportunity in your existing business will be determining the feasibility of your idea. Getting into the right business at the right time is simple advice, but advice that is sometimes difficult to implement. The high failure rate of new businesses and products (only 1 in 50 or 2% are found to be viable) indicates that very few ideas result in successful business ventures, even when introduced by well-established firms. Too many entrepreneurs start on a business venture, convinced of its merits, and then fail to thoroughly evaluate its potential. Time and money get wasted, and they become discouraged. The most common causes of "wrong starts" are:

- The idea is not well planned, especially in the area of knowing the market

- We have been dishonest with ourselves or enter with the wrong motives
- We lack the resolve to do all the hard work with the long hours
- We fail to seek or heed advice
- We get distracted with other pressing issues
- We don't have the needed resources
- We set unrealistic goals which then cause discouragement

Thus the need for the feasibility study. Some companies call this exercise "front end loading" (FEL). Carpenters and pipefitters say this simply as "measure twice, cut once." Jesus said "sit down and count the cost." No matter what it's called, it's a great idea to plan well.

What is a Feasibility Study?

As the name implies, a feasibility study is an analysis of the viability of an idea through gathering, analyzing and evaluating information and identifying potential problems with the purpose of answering the question: "Should I go into this business?" or "Is this idea viable?" If I go through with this business, will it live or die?

All activities of the study are directed toward helping answer this question before proceeding with the development of a business plan in order to save time, money and heartache later, on a business idea that did not work.

Preparing a feasibility study requires a tremendous amount of research and thinking which often leads to significant changes in the original idea. The good news is that the stronger the feasibility study the easier it is to develop your business plan and the more likely it is that your business will succeed.

1a. Phases-Preparation of a feasibility study involves 3 phases:

1. The collection of data (through research) which are relevant to all aspects of the undertaking;

2. The analyses of the collected data; and

3. The formulation of recommendations, based on the analyses.

1b. Goals– While too often a project study is merely considered as a procedural requirement for securing financing or government assistance, its real objective is to guide project promoters, business managers, and financial executives in determining the actions they must take on a business idea or a project in order to bring about its successful operation.

What is a feasible business idea? A feasible business venture is one where:

- The business will generate adequate cash-flow and profits,
- Survive the risks it will encounter,
- Remain viable in the long-term (sustainability) and
- Meet the goals of the founders.

This is the goal of the feasibility study: to evaluate a business idea and prove that it will meet these four (4) criteria. Overarching this is a determination to follow Biblical principles and to honor God in all that is done in setting up a "kingdom business."

1. What is the difference between a feasibility plan and a business plan?

2. A good feasibility plan will save you a LOT of time, heartache and money!

3. This study must be done before a business plan

Feasibility Study versus a Business Plan

A feasibility study is not a business plan. The separate roles of the feasibility study and the business plan are frequently misunderstood. Examine the comparison below.

	Feasibility Study	Business Plan
Primary Function	Provides an investigating function. It addresses the question of "Is this a viable business venture? Is it a good idea or not?"	Provides a planning function. Business plan outlines the actions needed to take the proposal from "idea" to "reality."
Alternatives Considered	Outlines and analyzes several alternatives or methods of achieving business success. The feasibility study helps to narrow the scope of the project to identify the best business scenario(s) three scenarios or alternatives.	Deals with only one alternative or scenario. This becomes the basis for the business plan.
Timing	Conducted before the business plan	Prepared only after business venture has been deemed to be feasible

If a proposed business venture is considered to be feasible, a business plan is usually constructed next that provides a "roadmap" of how the business will be created and developed. The business plan provides the "blueprint" for project implementation. If the venture is deemed not to be feasible, efforts may be made to correct its deficiencies, other alternatives may be explored, or the idea is dropped.

As shown in the diagram below, market research provides product/service information needed to conduct a feasibility study, which provides information and conclusions necessary to write a business plan. In Chapter 5, the development of a marketing and sales plan are combined.

Simplified Outline of a Feasibility Study or Plan

1. Cover Sheet
2. Executive Summary of the feasibility study
3. Description of the Product/Service
4. Market Feasibility
5. Technical Feasibility
6. Supply Chain and Leverage Feasibility
7. Safety Considerations
8. Spiritual Impact Feasibility
9. Organizational Feasibility
10. Financial Feasibility
11. Emotional Feasibility
12. Conclusions-do we move foreward, or not?

Use the three examples given in chapter 2, and discuss their feasibility in a roundtable discussion in class.

- Chicha morada, the purple corn drink
- Plastics reduced to oil for fuel
- Electrolysis of urine to produce light

Detailed Description of the Feasibility Study

Executive Summary – Summarizes key sections of the feasibility study. It should work as a separate, stand-alone document. Interested parties will read this section first in conjunction with a glance at the financial section when deciding whether or not they read the rest of the study. Key points to remember:

- Write this document after the content section of the study is completed.
- Although the Executive Summary is written last, it is presented first.
- It should be no more than one page long. More detail lessens the chances it will be read. It must convince the reader to put it on the top of their pile of reports!

Products and Services describes the products or services you intend to produce or deliver.

Describe the proposed business model or type of business. How will the business generate revenue? Manufacturing, merchandising or service provider?

Describe the business product or service in simple language. Give the product mix if the business will focus on more than one product.

How will the products or services be delivered?

What will be the business sector or category?

Market Feasibility uses the information learned from the Market Research to describe your target market, what characterizes that market, who the competition is, the advantage you will have over them, and how many products you expect your customers to buy.

Describe the general industry your business will operate within

What is the current market for your product or service (information from your previous market research)?

Who is your competition (information from your previous market research)? What will be your competitive advantage?

What is the anticipated future potential of your market? Will it increase in size, remain the same, or potentially decrease? By how much?

What is your target market? Who are the potential customers and what will be their primary benefit(s)?

How many products/services will you be able to sell (in the first year, second year), and for how much?

Technical Feasibility assesses the details of how you will produce and deliver a product or service (i.e., materials, labor, transportation, where your business will be located, technology needed, etc.). Think of the technical feasibility study as the logistical or tactical plan of how your business will produce, store, deliver, and track its products or services.

How will you produce your product? What technical or production challenges will you face?

What raw materials will you require and how will you obtain them?

How many people will be needed to produce the product or service? What skills will they need?

How will you deliver the product or service, and to whom (end customer, wholesaler, distributor)?

Example: A global restaurant chain constructed a supply factory in Eastern Europe to service their 10+ stores (restaurants) in their city. Since that time, about 5000 stores are in place across that country. (described in more detail in the discussion on supply chain in chapter 4)

Supply Chain Feasibility. Businesses often fail to produce the results expected or promised because of poorly planned supply chain. This section deals with where all raw materials come from, what the backup strategies need to be and how to optimize the supplies to assure that business isn't interrupted.

Safety Considerations. Safety in protecting both people and assets is not only the proper thing to do, it is good business. This section deals with how to address safety issues and protect your enterprise, no matter what that may be.

Spiritual Impact Feasibility. In what ways will your business be conducted so that people who do business with you and who work for you will know that you are a follower of God? How can you become well known in your community and be trusted?

Organizational Feasibility defines the legal and corporate structure of the business. It may also include professional background information about the founders and principals of the business and what skills they can contribute to the business.

What is your business or corporate structure? Do you have any operational principles or values that will be important to the business? Are you a technician, a manager or an entrepreneur? (see book by Michael Gerber in references)

What professional skills or experience do the leaders of the business provide?

Financial Feasibility predicts how much start-up capital is needed, sources of capital, and other financial considerations. It looks at how much cash is needed, where it will come from, and in general how it will be spent.

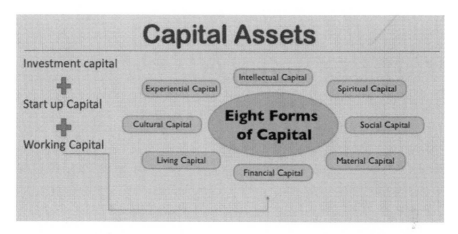

How much cash do you need to start your business and keep it running until it is self-sustaining?

How much cash will you need to maintain inside the business to keep it healthy?

Where will that start-up capital come from?

In general, how will the cash be spent in the first year? Second year?

What are your plans for accounts receivable, accounts payable and maintaining your inventory? Profit and loss accounting?

Emotional Feasibility. Are you emotionally ready to be responsible for a business? This is not often discussed in books, but it should be. Being in charge of your own business, or being put in a position of responsibility for a company for whom you work, requires the ability to endure some hardships, anxieties and frustrations which are usually never mentioned. Below is a list of some common, unexpected frustrations coming from a landlord who owns several shops:

- A delivery truck backs into your fence which now has to be repaired
- A tenant disappears one night and can't be found to pay that last 3 months' rent
- Another tenant has a fire which destroys not only his business but the adjoining ones. All of them face temporary loss of business, and it's "your fault!!"
- Another truck backs into a light pole and shuts the electric power off for your entire property
- One of the tenants is a restaurant which puts grease into the sewer used by every other tenant
- One tenant attracts a "bad crowd" which discourages other tenants' customers from doing business there and reduces the reputation of everyone.
- One tenant uses your property for non-business purposes
- You thought this was going to be a 5 or 6 day per week responsibility and it commands 24 hours a day, 7 days a week of your attention and you are tied to it.
- The list of frustrations are endless. Satisfaction in being a landlord is far from what you ever expected but now you are "stuck with it" and can't get free. The income is good, but is it really worth it? My family never sees me!
- Think about what frustrations could appear in your business. Are you ready?

Conclusions. In view of all of the above information, you must decide whether this is this a feasible business idea or not. What is an objective and realistic assessment of this business concept? Is this idea a "yes" or a "no"? Shall we keep the idea and revisit it later? Perhaps now is not the time considering all that we have learned.

Good Advice

Conducting a feasibility study as outlined above is good business practice. If you examine successful businesses, you will find that they did not go into a new business venture without first thoroughly examining all of the issues and assessing the probability of business success. Furthermore, it is good practice to do a 10-50-90 evaluation of the idea, which is illustrated below. The feasibility study is a critical step in the business assessment process. If properly conducted, it may be the best investment you'll ever make. Don't do all of it alone. Have committed friends to be part of your study. I especially encourage you to ask your spouse or loved ones to give their support and ideas, and take them seriously. Above all, pray earnestly and seek God's direction for what you should do.

Getting Started with Examples

The aqueduct from Hieropolis to Laodicea took millions of dollars to build and years of time. Once done, how well did it work?

The aqueduct of Laodicea (Revelation 3:14-16)

Two cities are described in the Bible (Colossians 4:13 and Revelation 3:14-16); Laodicea and Heiropolis. The town of Heiropolis was well known as the city with multiple warm springs and was a health resort for the Roman world at the time. It was positioned at higher elevation than Laodicea, which had nothing of the sort. About 21 km stood between the two towns and the people of Laodicea wanted to have their own hot springs! The Romans had become masters of aqueduct technology and it was well known how to build one which would transport water from the higher elevation to the lower.

Much planning, money and labor was devoted to getting such a structure constructed and the day finally came when warm waters could flow down to Laodicea. The happiness soon turned to dismay when the water which arrived at Laodicea was found to be neither hot nor cold, but only lukewarm. It was good for neither drinking nor bathing. It was salty and worthless! The project failed to meet its objectives because an adequate feasibility study was not done which would have shown that heat losses from the water transport were substantial. So much time, labor and money…wasted. When Revelation, the last book of the Bible, was written by Apostle John, it is no wonder that he used this example to describe the church at Laodicea condemning their lukewarmess toward God: "because you are lukewarm, neither hot nor cold, I am about to spit you out of my mouth." They knew exactly what He was talking about!

The famous Great Wall of China took over 2100 years to build, thousands of people to do it, starting in the Qin Dynasty in 700BC until the Ming Dynasty in about 1400AD.

The purpose of this marvelous piece of engineering, which has become a World Heritage Site, was to keep out marauding Mongol invasions from the north to protect the lives and treasures of the south. It was laid down brick by brick over very rugged terrain, and was so well done that much of it still exists today. But, did it work? After all that construction, it failed to work. The Mongols continued to maraude at will! How did they do it? Did the Mongols leap over the wall? No. Did they dig under the wall? No. Did they go around the wall? No. Did they break down the wall? Never! They found one or two corrupt gatekeepers who, for a "small fee", would leave the gates ajar at the preappointed time, and allow the Mongol hordes to go through. Would a good feasibility plan have prevented such a disappointment? It probably would have. But then, we wouldn't have one of the finest technical marvels in the world today! But it was not built as a tourist attraction.

The French Maginot Line was constructed at great cost and for a specific purpose; to prevent another invasion from Germany. The majority of World War I battles were fought on the French side of the border between France and Germany. At wars end, in 1918, that was deemed to be the war to end all wars. Never again would France suffer such an invasion! To insure that, they built what came to be known as the Maginot Line, a fortress of high-powered weapons situated along the entire border, facing in fixed positions toward Germany. Thousands of French soldiers, very large investment and much confidence was placed in this defensive position. However, when the Germans invaded again in 1940, they simply skirted the whole Maginot Line, going through Belgium instead, and left the line helpless to defend France. Several things went wrong here which would have been picked up in a good feasibility study:

- Times and technology change
- There might be another way to attack than a direct frontal assault along the border
- A good, well thought out "what if" study might have revealed the inadequacy of the line.
- Never underestimate the competition!
- Learn to expect the unexpected!

Solar cookers in Africa would seem to be a good idea. There is plenty of sun much of the time. But they don't work well in Saharan Africa. Why? In a laboratory, under "ideal" conditions, a solar cooker is perfect. It draws from the sun's energy to heat water, which cooks the food well. But in this part of the world, with sun in abundance, there is also wind in abundance. The blowing sand coats the panel and the energy available for cooking is much diminished. Setting up a solar cooker business may not work well in such an environment. How would a good feasibility study reveal potential problems?

This dog won't hunt!! This is an American expression meaning that something just isn't going to work. I was once assigned a job to build a factory production line for the separation of the 4 components of 2-liter plastic soft drink bottles. When I was given the job, a researcher had already done some work in his laboratory which showed that we needed a tank of special (somewhat hazardous and expensive) liquid which would allow one component to sink, and the other to float. Management was convinced that all I had to do was scale that idea up and 'voila' we would have a working factory! They gave me 3 months to put it all together. After seeing the laboratory demonstration, I felt the impracticability of this process. Nonetheless, anxious to please, I did my best to buy the right equipment and make it work. It was a failure. It didn't work, just as I had suspected it would not. Management was disappointed and I was embarrassed. The money I spent was wasted. I should have listened to my own advice and had the courage to speak up and tell them honestly that the process as originally proposed was not feasible and could never succeed and that I needed more time to start over and develop a better one. The original idea was technically not feasible. Nobody wants it!!

I was visited by a man and his wife in Peru. If looks could kill, he would be dead. The man's wife was furious with him and as he began to talk, I understood why. He introduced himself as a "builder", and had borrowed the full amount of several million dollars to construct a five-story apartment building in their city.

He had guaranteed the bank that he'd have the full amount repaid in 3 years by selling each of the five floors of high end, luxury apartments. The first floor sold immediately. The second floor also sold quickly. The third floor sold but with more effort. The fourth floor would not sell until he gave a sizable discount. The top floor would not sell at all. Nobody wanted it! The bank wanted their money. Why didn't it sell? The man had decided that the building didn't need an elevator for only five levels and that he could save money by not installing one. So now what to do?

The wife was desperate to put food on the table for the family, so her proposal was to become a seller for Mary Kay. She was sure that once she opened her cosmetics business, the Mary Kay company would give her a pink Cadillac which she could sell and use for family bills. The husband would hear none of that! "No wife of mine is going to...."!! His solution was to fly to Texas where there was plenty of work in construction, and in 3 months earn $3000. He didn't consider the fact that flying to Texas from Peru and back would cost about $1500 and living expenses there would be about $1000, so he'd leave his family for that long and bring back $500. What would you recommend that they do? How feasible were their plans? What was lacking?

Exercise

Discuss as a group the following four case studies, answering these three questions:

"Is this a viable business?"
"What is the problem?"
"What is the solution?"

Case A – Tobacco

A man from Ivory Coast was convinced that tobacco, of the kind used for cigar wrappers like that grown in Connecticut, could also be grown in his country. He studied how tobacco was planted, nourished and grown and became an expert on this part of agriculture. He bought land and a building near the area of Boundiali in western Ivory Coast, as the soil and the climate were ideal for the plants. He determined that it could be exported and that he could earn a good income, using inexpensive labor and some of the growing techniques he had learned. He invested $100,000.

His first crop grew very well in the ideal soil during a 4-month period. He harvested the leaves and hung them in the drying sheds. The tobacco turned to dust in a few days, and was unusable. He tried again and grew another crop. This time, the tobacco mildewed while hanging in the sheds, and was unusable. He eventually sold the land and the sheds for much less than he paid for it.

Problem

Ivory Coast may have great soil for tobacco, but it has only two seasons: hot and wet, and hot and dry. While it may grow well in the field, the critical part of preparing tobacco is how it is dried or cured. The climate was very ill-suited for that. If the tobacco cannot be cured, it has no value.

Solution

Before starting such a project, be certain that you know the entire process. In this case, being an expert in how to grow tobacco was not enough. He should have understood the entire production chain from where to buy the seeds or small plants, to techniques for planting to the curing process, to packaging, shipping and marketing, before making such an investment. A proper feasibility study would have revealed that tobacco production in this location would not work unless provision was made to cure the tobacco in a controlled environment, which would have cost much more money and made it unprofitable.

Poor basic data in the technical feasibility section (i.e. detailed understanding of how the entire process works) caused the downfall of this project.

Case B – Garments

A lady in the Ivory Coast is very skilled at making and sewing shirts, blouses, etc for the local populace. She measures the size for a customer, buys the textiles and can produce a shirt in about 3 days, selling it for about $10, beautifully custom made. She has been selling about 10 shirts per month. She uses an old sewing machine which has long since been paid off.

More and more, this lady is asked to make shirts which have embroidery on them. She does not have the machine for that, and has to outsource the embroidery to another person in town who charges her so much that she makes little profit on the shirt in the final analysis. So she has refused to take many customer orders.

Would it be feasible for her to invest in a $500 embroidery machine and do that work herself?

She studied the local market and determined that if she had an embroidery machine, she could make 10 additional shirts per month and sell them for $15 each. She already has a good reputation and by offering this new ability, her reputation would be enhanced. This is the financial feasibility calculation she needed to go forward to seek money for another machine:

	Situation Now	Diff	Proposed Position
Shirts/month	10	10	20
Selling price, $/shirt	10	15	12.50
Revenue, $/month	100	150	250
Itemized Costs			
Textiles, cloth,$/mo.	50	50	100
Embroidery, $/mo.	0	10	10
Thread, $/mo.	5	5	10
Buttons, $/mo.	5	5	10
Electricity, $/mo.	5	5	10
Salaries, $/mo.	20	20	40
Int capital loan, $/mo	0	5	5
Total, $/month	85	100	185
Gross Income $/mo (Rev-Csts)	15	50	65
Taxes Gross Income, $/mo	2	4	6
Net income.$/month	13	46	59

Net Income $/year	156	552	708
New Capital Needed $	0	500	500
Net return new capital, %	0	110%	
Payback new capital in months	0	11	

Problem (or opportunity)

She found herself unable to meet the demand for a different kind of clothing and could not meet that demand without an investment.

Solution

By carefully considering the market, the finances and her own abilities, she decided to obtain a loan of $500, and wrote her business plan accordingly. This was indeed feasible. She agreed to a capital loan payback in which she made only a small profit on the new machine during the first three years, but once it was paid off, she saw greatly increased profits.

Comments

This could be viewed as an example of a 'mix-enrichment' program, in which you choose to add to your assets and produce a higher value product within the existing business.

This example could also have been viewed as a 'make versus buy' decision since she could have not made a new investment, and instead decided to outsource the embroidered garments which would have cost her more, but she would have kept most of her customers. What were other alternatives she might have chosen?

Exercise

Given the information above, determine what the lady's cash flow will be in the next five years, with the first year being the year in which the investment is made in the new embroidery machine, and assuming a 36-month payback on the $500 loan.

	Today's situation	Year 1	Year 2	Year 3	Year 4	Year 5
Capital, $	0	170	170	160	0	0
Net Income,$/year	156	708	708	708	708	708
Net Cash Flow, $/year	156	538	538	538	708	708
Cumulative Cash Flow, $	156	694	1232	1770	2308	2846

Note: This example reminds us of the master who gave sums of money to each of three servants, to invest for him and earn a profit while he was away. When he came back, he demanded to know what the servants had done with his money. This lady would have a good answer, would she not? (This is a true story based on presenting these principles in 2013 in Korhogo, Cote d'Ivoire).

What could she consider doing after the third year, once the loan is paid off? Perhaps yet a third machine? What would be the implications of such an expansion plan?

A final note is the nature of the three-column presentation used above to compare costs. It represents only a "snapshot" in time, usually done to show the third year of a proposed change in the operation. Therefore, it is of limited value. The real value of this calculation is the detailed cost analysis. That should be calculated for each year and will change from year to year. A more robust analysis is presented in the cash flow presentation which begins before the new investment and goes forward about five years readily showing the payback time, which is most important. Preferably, this should be done month by month, or quarter by quarter, then summed up in annual terms. The payback time is shown as 3 years, but that can be seen as a choice more than a necessity. She does make enough money with the new line of clothing to pay the whole loan back in the first year. If she did that, she would save some interest payments. But by spreading her loan repayments over three years, she is protecting herself against some slow starts with the new machine, or an overall business slowdown.

Case C - Making Jewelry in Nepal

A lady wants to go into the business of making necklaces, bracelets, etc. She knows where to buy many of the components cheaply. Other components which are not locally available can be bought from importers who trek the mountains over the border with China. She also has a supply of other ladies who are able to help her, and who need a part time job desperately.

In going through a feasibility study, she comes to these conclusions:

Feasibility Study.

Cover sheet : "Hand-made jewelry from Nepal"

Executive Summary: one page, stating that the business will generate a profit within the first year of operation

Description of products and services: many designs of necklaces, bracelets and pins

Market Feasibility: there is competition, but there is a demand for superior quality

Technical Feasibility: no question, we can make such products and do so without highly technical equipment

Supply Chain Feasibility: Almost all of her supplies come across the Himalayas from merchants. Does she feel safe with that arrangement? What degree of leverage did she have over her suppliers, the volume, their prices, the weather…anything?

Spiritual Impact Feasibility: She can indeed have an impact on her workers and her customers by treating them fairly and other forms of witness.

Safety Feasibility: There is nothing dangerous about this operation, and the neighborhood in which she intends to locate is a low crime area.

Organizational Feasibility: The owner can hire the right people and keep a good workforce which can increase or decrease depending on the sales

Financial Feasibility: A cash flow analysis indicates that within the first six months, the business should be profitable. To get started, borrowed money is needed.

Conclusion and recommendations: The necessary money should be borrowed, and it can be paid back within the following two years

Problem

After three years, sales were still not enough to be able to pay back the money borrowed from a bank to get started. This was due to four unexpected reasons:

1. The location was not on a tourist thoroughfare, and the passersby were not customers

2. Making connections with foreigners who would order jewelry in bulk quantities was difficult

3. The sources from wandering merchants was unreliable and the store often didn't have the wide choices of raw materials they needed to make good products

4. The ladies whom the owner hoped to hire, proved to be unreliable too, and would not show up to work on time, or would simply quit, and she would have to train new people all the time.

Solution

A more thorough feasibility study should have been done, and it would have revealed that these problems could be avoided by locating in a place more frequented by tourists with money to spend. It would have also revealed that it would be necessary to keep a larger inventory of raw materials so that, when the supplies varied, they would have something to work with. A closer look at the value chain and supply chain was needed.

The value chain and supply chain

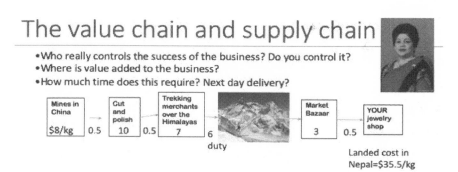

- Who really controls the success of the business? Do you control it?
- Where is value added to the business?
- How much time does this require? Next day delivery?

Mines in China		Cut and polish		Trekking merchants over the Himalayas			Market Bazaar		YOUR jewelry shop
$8/kg	0.5	10	0.5	7	6		3	0.5	

duty

Landed cost in Nepal=$35.5/kg

This example is a good one to talk about control and value. There are two important questions which apply to all businesses:

1. Who really controls the success of the business? Did she control it?
2. Where is value added to the business?

75

Where are her points of leverage in which she has any control over aspects of her business? Looking at this supply chain diagram, there are very few areas of leverage.

In addition, when the border between China and Nepal is crossed, the merchants must pay a duty amounting to 0.5 $/kg

By the time the goods reach the jewelry shop, the accumulated value is 35.5 $/kg

Over which steps in her supply chain does she have control?

In which steps in this supply chain is your business the most vulnerable?

In which steps of the supply chain is the cost significantly increased?

If one or two of these steps failed, or doubled in price, what backup plan do you have to survive in your business?

Do your competitors use the same supply chain, or a different one? If so, what is it?

The costs do not stop accumulating at 35.5$/kg. The following must be added:

- Trip to the bazaar assume that is no cost (is this a good assumption?)
- Cost to advertise   2 $/kg
- Cost to sell the products   2 $/kg
- Taxes paid on the operation of the store; assume that is no cost (is this a safe assumption?)
- Cost of labor to assemble the jewelry   5 $/kg
- Cost of salaries (the owner primarily)   5 $/kg
- Cost to rent the building   2 $/kg
- Cost to package the finished goods   2 $/kg

The total cost of finished goods, ready to offer the customers is 54 $/kg

What profit margin do you expect based on competitive pricing in your area? 6 $/kg

The selling price should then be 60 $/kg, generating a 10% profit margin.

Notice how important it is to reduce each cost element to the same units. If one is $/month, and the other is $/kg, and yet another is $/square meter, you can't draw any conclusions from that.

Express every item in the same, consistent units!

Case D - Taking Care of the Elderly in Philadelphia

The younger generation of people who have moved to Philadelphia from other countries look forward to succeeding in getting a good paying job once they graduate from one of the several fine universities in this city. Once a job is secured, they often bring their parents and/or grandparents to live with them. Often, however, these elders do not speak English and miss the companionship of people their age back in the homeland. While the younger people work all day, the elders sit at home and are quite lonely, watching TV they don't understand. This business provides a place for daily care for the elders. This "elder day care home" provides a bus to pick up the elders and bring them to the home, then take them back to their children's homes at night, operating five days per week. The charge is a daily fee of $75/day, and is in part supported by the local government. The elders talk, play games, read, relax, have lunch all in an environment in which they converse with folks their own age who speak the same language and who share similar life experiences. There is a nurse on duty just in case a problem arises. When the elders return home at night, they are content and smiling! (and ready for bed)! It is a win-win situation. The younger people are happy that the elders are well cared for, and the elders are happy with the home and all the friends their age. The home operates five days/week.

Exercises – Executive Summaries

Exercises I

Using the jewelry example, make up a cost and income sheet like that above in the garment example (Case B). List all of your assumptions.

Exercise II

Continuing to use the jewelry example, make up a cash flow sheet like that above in the garment example (Case B). List all of your assumptions.

Exercise III

Do a "sanity check" on exercises I and II. Is this the best you can do? Does this really make sense? What assumptions have I made which could mean trouble ahead?

1. List the essential elements of a feasibility plan down the left-hand side of the paper and write brief answers on the right side
2. Name of your company
3. Product or service
4. Market feasibility
5. Technical feasibility
6. Supply Chain feasibility
7. Organizational feasibility
8. Spiritual Impact feasibility
9. Safety feasibility
10. Financial feasibility
11. Conclusions and recommendations
12. What could go wrong and what would you do if it did go wrong? What's your "Plan B"?

Once you have finished, form small groups of four or five, and discuss what you have each done and learned in these exercises. Share you assumptions.

On the next pages are two examples of an executive summary of a feasibility plan, both using the jewelry shop as an example, and the short list shown above earlier as "Hand-made jewelry from Nepal"
. Such a report could be presented to possibly interest a future partner or investor. Do they contain all of the elements in a compelling way? What could be deleted or added?

FEASIBILITY SUMMARY (using jewelry In Nepal example)

Hand-Made Jewelry From Nepal

The feasibility of this idea has been well investigated and judged to be strong. Based on our studies, the business should be profitable after the first year, generating a 10% profit margin. This will be done by making and selling many varieties of necklaces, bracelets, pins and hair adornments for ladies and gentlemen, which will represent the unique styles of Nepal, using locally available materials.

Our workforce will be local artisans who are eager to find new jobs. And the quality of their work is excellent. While there is competition, our market study concludes that there is plentiful market here in Nepal for both local citizens sold retail and in bulk quantities sold wholesale worldwide. We plan to serve both markets.

We focused on our supply chain as a critical element of our success and sustainability, and have found that while the quality of the goods coming from China is excellent, we must have a more stable supply. Therefore, we know where other goods can be purchased at reasonable prices and without the risks carried by just one supplier. We feel greater assurance of supply with more than one source.

We plan to rent facilities in which to work and since there is no equipment needed, but only space, we need no permanent capital. We need to have a supply of money to pay the rent, buy raw materials, and to pay the initial salary and utility costs before we get income from sales. Our goal is to pay back this initial operations loan as quickly as possible.

Having a strong spiritual impact on our workers and community is a very high goal and we know how to do that. The safety of this operation is also assured by the good training that we expect to give to our employees.

Overall, we submit this plan as a highly feasible one, in which we have examined all of the needed steps and know that we can achieve the goals on the timetable of start up by six months from time of the loan, and payback of operating cash loans by the second year.

Respectfully Submitted for your consideration and support, "the team". Date:

Royal Jewelry Company Feasibility

The name for the proposed business is the "Royal Jewelry Company", located in Banepa, Nepal.

A team of five people met during the last year to discuss and test the feasibility of establishing a small business for the purpose of making high quality jewelry typical of the area, yet affordable to many people. While some may be sold to people who come to the area, the main customers will be those in foreign countries who will buy from us wholesale, and then sell it retail in such places as the EU, the USA and the Middle East. To do this, we have arranged for wholesale representatives in those regions who will gain a royalty of 10% of the profit which we will realize on the products. In order to maintain good service, we will make our products to inventory a 2-month supply of many styles and be ready to ship these to the wholesale representatives with little delay.

Technically, we have the resources to make any style of jewelry that the wholesalers ask for and we will keep up with the trends using these people as guides. There is a good supply of skilled personnel where our factory is located. The supply of basic raw materials has been a concern but has been resolved by opening up two other sources of all raw materials. These new supply sources are in country and not as susceptible to bad weather, shipping distance or international trade issues. In total, we will maintain three sources of all supplies. Our organization is strong in keeping the management team flat, treating all employees equally as "associates", giving workers bonuses periodically, and expecting a low turnover rate because our wages are quite competitive and working conditions are good. As a Christian business, we see the feasibility of having a good impact on the community and the workers, by freely advertising that we are a company which is based on Biblical principles or fair treatment to workers and customers alike.

This plan is financially feasible because a substantial amount of such jewelry has already been made and sold to local people and visitors from abroad. Based then on feasible marketing, demonstrated technology and a good skill base, and by careful calculations for fixed and variable cost control, demand and selling prices, we believe it is feasible to earn profit margins of 10 to 20%, pre-tax, over total costs.

This study group has concluded that this proposed company is feasible and the preparation of a formal business plan should begin.

Some possible questions could come from those who show interest in this idea (it is NOT YET a business plan because there are no financial numbers in it yet):

Suppose the estimated size of the market drops due to larger companies offering the same products. What will you do then?

Are you being conservative or overly optimistic in your market size?

Can you confirm that there is no significant competition for your product at this time, either from Nepal or another country which will undercut your prices?

Would you consider taking on any partners?

Have you had any discussions with potential wholesalers yet, and if so, what were the results?

With a local retail business, there are only minor concerns about shipping costs and customs and paying duties. With this proposed wholesale business, you will be shipping large quantities across borders. This involves more expense in freight that retail didn't involve, and more paperwork. Must you insure against loss of a shipment?

Compare this feasibility summary with the outline given as "Hand-made jewelry from Nepal." Many concerns were left unanswered.

The summary resolves several of the issues. First, the name has been changed to give a more appealing, more exotic, less common impression. Second, the marketing scheme has been totally revised. It no longer matters where the factory is located, although some local business is expected. The primary focus is foreign wholesale, not local retail. This will shift the focus on "make to inventory", rather than "make to order", so that larger amounts can be shipped. There is a world of difference between selling retail and selling wholesale. There is no mention of how invoicing and payment can take place. Getting paid for products and services is a problem everywhere in the world, and dependence on markets far away is more risky. This needs to be carefully studied and explained in the business plan. Another important change from the original plan is securing the supply chain by opening up three suppliers of all of the basic goods, rather than depending on only one. While the quality and the prices from the original supplier were good, there were so many risk factors which indicated that this business could be left waiting and have little control, that it could have doomed the business.

What is left to do? The initial economics have not been thoroughly studied and there is therefore no mention of how much capital is needed, and for what purpose, or how much capital of various kinds needs to be borrowed. There is also no discussion about how the bills will be paid, in either scenario. Knowing that cash must be kept in the business to maintain financial health, how will the company do that if they must pay for large amounts of raw material inventory and not get the money back for a long time until the goods are made and sold to the wholesaler? Will the owners of this business purchase on credit or cash? If purchases are on a cash basis, then there has to be cash available, especially at times when there appears a lower price for the goods. If payment is on a credit basis, then there are time limits for repayment, beyond which interest begins to accrue. Will the customers pay the business in cash, or on credit? Many businesses I am familiar with suffer with customers who take the goods and services and withhold payment, making some excuse why they don't have the money right now.

Examining both documents above, which would you say is best, more compelling and demanding more work be done because it shows such promise? Why do you choose the one over the other?

Are the owners of this business content with being solely responsible to borrow all of the money needed, or are they willing to give some of the equity of the business to the lender? For example, a lender may be willing to loan the full amount needed and offer marketing help in return for 20% of the ownership of the business. If wholesale is the best way to make money, then having someone who has connections and a network through which to make sales would be vital.

Chapter 4 Business Plan

Subject:	Your Business Plan
Lesson Objectives:	Understand what a business plan is and how it helps in the development of a business
	Create a business plan that builds on the feasibility study recently completed
	Participants will develop their own business plan, and defend it to the instructors
Books recommended	"The Everything Business Plan Book", Ramsey and Windhaus

Introduction

You have completed a feasibility study, in which you examined several alternative businesses and chosen one of them. You asked yourself "is this a viable business for me (us) to enter?" Feasibility studies are conducted before the business plan to help you focus on which business to enter, and when. Now, having established that, you are ready to work on your business plan.

Your business must be built on a firm foundation that will last. Scripture tells us:

"Everyone who hears these words of mine and puts them to practice is like a wise man who builds his house on a rock…when storms come, it does not fall…but a foolish man builds his house on sand…and when the storms come, it will fall" (Matthew 7:24-27)

This business plan is an essential part of that foundation. We are taught to first sit down and count the cost of any venture before we start it:

"Suppose one of you wants to build a tower. Will he not first sit down and estimate the cost to see if he has enough money to complete it?" (Luke 14:28-30)

This is the exercise we are to begin right now.

- The Elements of a Business Plan
- Your Executive Summary, written last, presented first.
- Background Information
- The concept of your business
- A brief description of your background
- Your mission statement
- How you will market your business and sell your products
- Your operations plan, including quality control and production capability
- How much capital, and what kinds of capital, over how much time, will you need?
- Your social and spiritual impact plan
- Your safety plan. How will you protect your business, employees and customers?
- Your financial plan, which includes your cost analyses, cash flow estimates, payback, and your assessment of risk.

Your business plan will go through several iterations as you write it. For example, it could be:

A rough draft (50% completed assuming half of it will be changed when you write it again)

A copy for review by outsiders and team members (about an 85% level of accuracy)

The final draft that you use to manage your start-up and give to the funding partners

Your business plan is meant to be a working document, not one just to sit on a shelf.

Now we will describe each of the elements above in greater detail.

Your Executive Summary

An executive summary is a short summary (1 page maximum) of the main points and concepts of your business plan. Its purpose is to allow anyone reading the business plan to get a brief introduction to your business and the strategic parts of your plan. This document is the first to be presented to potential lenders, although it is the last document written because it is based on all the information which has been collected.

Background Information. The Concept of Your Business

What is your business concept? You addressed this in your field research and the feasibility study, so in this section you summarize answers to any or all of the following questions:

- What is the main product or service?
- How is there a market for my business?
- Who is my target customer? Who are other potential customer groups?
- How will we produce our product or deliver our service?
- What are the key people and resources we need to succeed?
- What are my personal, financial, social, and spiritual goals for this business?

A Brief Description of Your Background

This section addresses the experience, skills and training of you and your start-up team. It demonstrates why you have what is necessary to succeed in this endeavor. You do this by introducing all of the key start-up personnel along with a description of their skills, experience, capacity, any limitations or conflicts of interest, etc.

Your Mission Statement/Slogan

A mission statement tells the public why you exist as a company. It generally describes who your target customer is, what your business will do for them, and how you will do it. These statements create an idea about you and your company in the minds of those who work for you, your customers, and your potential customers. Mission statements need to be easy to memorize and clear in meaning.

Here are some examples of key phrases from corporate mission statements, or corporate mottoes which companies want customers to remember easily:

- Better things for better living, through chemistry (DuPont Company-no longer used) chemicals, plastics, specialty fibers
- Do it once and do it right (Process Systems & Design, Inc.) engineering design
- We save people money so they can live better. (Walmart)
- Our mission is to make Target the preferred shopping destination for our guests by delivering outstanding value, continuous innovation and an exceptional guest experience. Expect More. Pay Less. (Target, a general product discount store)
- We deliver! Linde Chemical
- Quality is Job One. Ford Motor Company cars
- Think. IBM Corporation electronics
- Don't be evil. Google information technology
- Impossible is nothing! Adidas shoes
- The power of dreams. Honda cars
- Finger Lickin' Good! KFC restaurant franchise chain
- Because I'm worth it. L'Oreal cosmetics
- I'm lovin' it. McDonalds restaurant franchise chain
- Be everywhere, do everything and never fail to astonish the customer. Macy's
- The Goal is Zero. DuPont Safety slogan
- Eat Mor Chikin. Chick-Fil-A restaurant franchise chain

Which do you think are too short or too long, too difficult to memorize, or too unclear in their meaning? What immediate impression does each one give you of the company it represents?

Which is the best one in your opinion? Write your comments below. Write a few ideas for a motto for your own business which represents who you are and what you offer to your customers. Remember to be culturally aware! The Chevrolet "Nova" didn't prove to be too popular in Mexico because it means "no go" in Spanish. The Ford "Pinto" sounds intriguing in American parlance, but among macho men in Brazil, it didn't sell because it insults private parts! Who wants to buy a "pinto"?

A great expression of a Christian company's business goal is Correct Craft, Inc. Orlando, FL, which builds pleasure boats of many designs. Their mission statement, in a triangle is:

What is your opinion of that stated goal for the business, operated by Christians?

Below is a good example of a mission statement from a restaurant named "The Well", in Hockessin, Delaware. It is a separate business entity owned by a nearby church.

"It is our goal at the Well to provide our community with a place where people find quality service to go along with quality products. All profits from The Well go to local and global missions, helping children, families and people in need. SO, by allowing us to serve you, you are helping us to serve others. How cool is that?"

How You Will Market Your Business and Sell Products

You must have a marketing and sales plan. You must know how you will let potential customers know about your business and sell your products/services. In your market research and feasibility study you described your target market, what characterized that market, who your competition is, the advantage you will achieve over them, and an estimate of how many products and/or services you expected your customers to buy. Now in the business plan you need to propose a plan of specific steps you will take to achieve those product or service goals. This part of the business plan involves both marketing and sales planning and projections.

The difference between marketing and sales:

Marketing- knowing and analyzing the market for your goods, understanding the trends (where is the need for your product or service going in the short term and long term), how you will price your product/service, and how you will let potential customers know about your products (often called promotion)

Sales- the process of interacting with customers, negotiating their decision to buy, and making sure that what they bought gets delivered on time and in good condition, whether that is a product or a service.

Your marketing plan should answer any or all of the following questions for at least the first year of business:

How will you continually keep in touch with your market and customer needs?

What future trends in your product/service do you need to consider?

How will you price your product/service?

What specific promotional ways will you use to let customers know of your product/service (marketing campaigns or methods such as advertising, word-of-mouth, referrals, etc.).

Your sales plan should describe your:

Customer Service Process: The way in which you want to interact with your customers

Sales Process: How you will influence a customer to make a decision to buy

Distribution Process: How you will deliver the product or service

Will it be delivered on the spot, shipped from your own facility, or shipped from someone else's facility?

Will the product be readily available in inventory or will you produce it once you have an order?

The end result of your sales and marketing plan should be a table of marketing activities and product sales projections (in quantity and sales dollars) extended out for at least three years, preferably five years.

These projections will be an estimate, but they need to be as reasonable and justifiable as possible.

Month-by-month projections are more accurate than just projecting annual sales. They can show seasonal variations too.

Your sales projections are more useful if you make monthly projections that fit at least two scenarios (three Is better):

1. Expected case (average projections that have a 50% probability of succeeding and a 50% chance of failing).
2. Worst case (lowest possible projections that have a 90% chance of being met or exceeded)
3. Best case (highest possible projections that have a 10% chance of being met or exceeded)

Here's an example of such a sales projection for a palm oil manufacturer (we are only showing yearly projections but your plan should have month-by-month projections as the basis):

PROJECTED SALES OF PALM OIL, TONS PER YEAR

Full year of operation	1	2	3	4	5
10% chance	103	130	160	190	220
50% chance	74	100	130	160	190
90% chance	58	80	110	140	170

Each of these scenarios needs to be examined in your financial plan for cost and profitability impact. Can your business succeed if the first three years of its operation follows the 50% projection? Most successful start-up businesses assume the 50% chance scenario, but plan for the 90% chance scenario.

Perhaps you should consider the 10% chance scenario too. If business exceeds your expectations, will you have to turn away customers because you cannot produce that much? Will producing that much require additional capital? Your request for capital needs to be consistent with what that capital, once installed and started up, can produce!

Note: You will notice that 'clarity of vision' is characteristic of the first year, but that is less so in the years that follow. This is typical. The latter years are your best "educated" guess, but based on prayer and sound judgement.

An essential component of the sales projection is the selling price projection. Do the same kind of analysis for the price of the product that you plan to sell, and be sure that you are going to survive if the price drops below what you planned. Here is an example, based on the palm oil.

PROJECTED SELLING PRICE OF PALM OIL, $/TON

Full year of operation	1	2	3	4	5
10% chance	795	810	830	850	870
50% chance	679	700	720	740	760
90% chance	521	540	580	620	640

As with sales volume, the sales price in the business plan will be based on the 50% chance scenario. However, it is very wise to analyze what will happen to your business if either of the other chances occur. Can your business survive if a competitor drops the price and you are forced to do the same? How low can the price fall and still make a profit? How long can you sustain your business if the price falls to the 90% chance point, and remains there for several months or years? What will you do if that happens?

People invested in petroleum in 2014 when the price commanded in the $140/barrel range. Soon thereafter, the price dropped into the $80/barrel range, and then kept dropping. It's present price point is about $50/barrel, in 2019. Will it ever go back to the $100/barrel range? The volume demand remained, but the price has been shattered!

Your Operations Plan

- An operations plan describes the processes you will use to produce the product or service and other business processes necessary to support the company and employees. It addresses any of the following processes or operations that are appropriate:
- Product manufacturing or service delivery
- Information management, communications and technology
- Staffing needs and training
- Financial management and budgeting
- Planning and scheduling
- Warehouse and shipping
- Marketing and sales
- Part time help, interns and contractors

There will be a later lesson in this series that will explain more in detail how you plan the different operational processes.

The Capital You Will Need

Where will you get the capital to start this enterprise? How much money do you need? There are three categories of capital that you need to consider at this time:

Investment capital- the money to buy and install equipment, buildings, design, etc. These are "hard assets" which could be later sold with the selling of the business if you decided to do that. These hard assets should be insured against loss.

Startup cost- the money to buy your first raw materials (to use for training labor how to run the equipment), do analyses, hire a consultant, etc. This is money you have to spend in order to begin your operation. It is "sunk money" that you are probably never getting back.

Working capital- the money to buy inventory, raw materials, spare parts, etc. on an ongoing basis. This is money you have invested but have not gotten back yet, but will get back when you make and sell the goods that come from it.

Every type of business has a different requirement for cash. Here are some examples:

- Business A is to make necklaces and other jewelry
- Business B is to process, package and sell palm oil
- Business C is to counsel business people in how to make their business better
- Business D is to operate a taxi business in your town

Business Type	A	B	C	D
Investment capital	Very low	Very high	Very low	Medium
Startup cost	Very low	Medium	Very low	Low
Working capital	High	Medium	Very low	Low

Later in this training book there will be an entire lesson on how to raise capital. For the purposes of writing this section of your business plan, your plan needs to specify:

1) how much of each kind of capital you will need, 2) when you will need it, and 3) where it will come from (sources).

Where does capital come from? The traditional way to find the capital you need to start your business is from the national banking system. Banks will vary in how easily they will lend money, and how much they will lend, and what interest rate they will charge.

There are many types of loans, including fixed rate, variable rate, secured and unsecured, simple interest rate and other payback plans. There are other lending institutions which are set up as microloans and venture capitalists, private investors who will loan you money to begin your business. Finally, many people either put together a partnership in which they all contribute money and then expect a share of the profits, or there is a private investor who will hold your loan and expect a return. One purpose of this book is to help you convince a lending institution or investor group to loan you money.

There are many ways to get money in the world, varying by culture. In some countries, particularly western cultures, the decision to participate in a loan is driven by numbers. How accurate do the numbers seem to be and how confident in them are you? Can you convince your potential lenders to be confident too? In other parts of the world, an established, personal relationship is an essential prerequisite for loaning or buying into a business.

Your Social and Spiritual Impact Plan

Your business will have a message to the community in which you live. What is that message? Here are some examples of the "message" that some businesses have in their communities:

- "those people are rude!" (not a desirable message to be broadcast about your company!)
- "they always seem ready to help me find what I need."
- "they always seem to understand me"
- "they must be Christians because they treat me well as their customer"
- "they always seem to have what I need."

A large plant (US Plastic Corp) located on Interstate 75 in Lima, Ohio leaves no doubt by displaying one large sign on the building. In well lighted letters for everyone to see from the highway, the sign reads "Christ is the Answer". The owner, Stanley Tam, often says "my business is a pulpit from which I tell about the love of Christ!" Dr.Tam has given over $140 million to the Christian work around the world. He began with $25 in his pocket, and built the business to over $100 million. Dr. Tam has formally, legally transferred the ownership from himself to God, over the objections of several lawyers.

A social and spiritual impact plan takes into consideration: The many different groups of people that can be spiritually influenced by your business (employees, families of employees, suppliers, customers, and even the community).

God Owns My Business

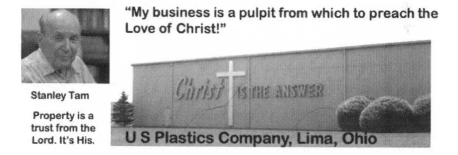

"My business is a pulpit from which to preach the Love of Christ!"

Stanley Tam

Property is a trust from the Lord. It's His.

U S Plastics Company, Lima, Ohio

Intentional spiritual conversations with people that are connected with the business as well as evangelistic and discipleship activities throughout the year.

Your social and spiritual impact plan discusses these issues and develops specific commitments, processes, and metrics that seek to develop the second and third bottom lines of your business. What kind of reputation, or message, do you want to have in your community?

One company adopted the name LYNAYS, which is not a word in any dictionary but opens the question about its meaning. "Love Your Neighbor as Your Self". It is an electrical company located in Abidjan, Cote d'Ivoire whose 20 employees serve needs in the entire country. They, like the owner, treat customers lovingly as Christians should.

Your safety assurance plan

How will you assure and protect the safety and preservation of your business' permanent assets, your people and your customers in a way that nothing shuts you down or takes you to court, so that every customer can count on you as a reliable source or supplier? Safety is good business, as well as humanitarian behavior!

Your Financial Plan

Your financial plan uses the data in previous sections of your business plan (such as the marketing, sales, operations, and capital plans) and from your feasibility study, to make a detailed projection of the financial condition of the company over the first three years of operation.

Many business plans contain a budget that estimates projected income, expenses, and profit/loss for the first three years. This is helpful, but a start-up entrepreneur needs more precise financial information that not only projects month-by-month income and expenses, but also can project cash flow and the maximum amount of capital the business will need. Only a cash flow projection can do that. Many start-up businesses fail because they run out of cash (even though on paper they may be making a profit). Therefore, your best financial plan is a three-year, month-by-month cash flow projection. Stronger yet, make it a five-year projection!

A cash flow projection has four basic parts:

1. Beginning cash balance. - Your cash at the start of the period (month, year, etc.)
2. Sources of funds (inflow) – Where inflow of cash would come from during the period.   Examples: sales of products and/or services, donations, loans, etc.
3. Utilization of funds (outflow) - Where cash would be spent (outflow) during the period.   Examples: raw materials, salaries, equipment, rent, etc.

4. Ending cash balance – Balance of your cash at the end of the period

Every cash flow projection has the following basic formula: Beginning cash balance + Sources of funds (inflow) - Utilization of funds (outflow) = Ending cash balance

As you put together your cash flow estimate, you must be very realistic. This will require that you not work alone, but have people whom you can trust to check your work, and help you with the reality and accuracy of the numbers. This is extremely important because it shows you how your business will behave and you do not have any unpleasant surprises. It is also a basis for appearing before potential lenders, and partners, and they will make their judgments about whether to support you or not, based on your cash flow. You will get many questions about your assumptions, so you must be prepared to answer them. One of the questions you will get is about the risks you are taking, and where risks appear in your cash flow estimate.

Advice: Learn to shield your downside risk by having backup plans. What if your sales projections are low? What if your raw material costs go up unexpectedly? What if a significant or key employee quits the job suddenly? What if a competitor moves in right across the street? What if you become ill?

Hold a risk summit. This is a key meeting in which your principle partners get together to assess what the risks (like those described above) might be.

Carefully itemize the capital costs you will need. The more detail, the better.

Avoid bad surprises in your business. Do not shake the confidence of your investors.

You will be asked to keep and show your profit and loss sheets. How much has come in during a given month or quarter, and how much has gone out. Keep careful accounting of these month by month, and let the bottom line show either a positive or a negative result. The key to this is to be totally honest so that you truly know what Is happening. Some months will show once a quarter or annual payments which will make that particular month look badly, but that is fine. Honesty. accuracy and thoroughness are the keys. If this isn't done properly, you will be blind in knowing where your business is in a given month or quarter.Here is a sample of the first year's projected cash flow for a start-up business. Your cash flow projection will be much more involved. This projection starts by assuming no capital has been raised for the business.

	Jan	Feb	March	April	May	June
Beginning cash	0	-200	-700	-1,200	-1,400	-1,900
Sales	0	0	0	100	150	200
Capital raised	0	0	0	0	0	0
Total inflow	0	0	0	100	150	200
Product material	0	250	200	0	400	0
Marketing	0	50	100	100	50	50
Salaries	75	75	75	75	75	75
Rent	100	100	100	100	100	100
Utilities	25	25	25	25	25	25
Total outflow	200	500	500	300	650	250
Ending cash bal	-200	-700	-1,200	-1,400	-1,900	-1,950

	July	Aug	Sept	Oct	Nov	Dec
Beginning cash	-1,950	-2,375	-2,100	-2,200	-2,275	-2,050
Sales	300	500	550	500	800	800
Capital raised	0	0	0	0	0	0
Total inflow	300	500	550	500	800	800
Product material	500	0	325	350	300	400
Marketing	0	0	50	0	50	0
Salaries	100	100	100	100	100	100
Rent	100	100	100	100	100	100
Utilities	25	25	25	25	25	25
Total outflow	725	225	650	575	575	625
Ending cash bal	-2,357	-2,100	-2,200	-2,275	-2,050	-1,875

Notice some of the things we can learn from this cash flow projection:

In any start-up business, cash outflow precedes inflow. In other words, you start spending money before you ever earn money.

In a new business, positive cash flow (where cash inflow exceeds outflow in a given month) may not occur until later in the first year, or even in the second year. In this example, positive cash flow only starts in November.

By building the initial cash flow projection for the business assuming no capital has been raised, the worst-case ending cash balance (-2,375 in July) is the amount of capital that will need to be raised to keep the business from going into a cash-deficit situation in the first year. That is the amount of capital that your projection tells you that you need to raise minimum before you start your business.

Anyone who loans you money to either invest or start up, will want to know when they will get their money back. You do that with a three-year cash flow projection. They will ask you what are the risks of this not happening, Your answers to when and how much, will be answered in a chart like this one below:

	Year 1	Year 2	Year 3
Beginning cash balance	50	-3200	-2400
Sale of merchandise	100	4000	8000
Capital raised	1000	0	50
Total inflow	1100	4000	8050
Product materials	2000	1000	1500
Marketing expense	500	300	300
Salaries (including yours)	700	700	800
Rent	800	800	800
Utilities	300	400	600
Loan interest	50	50	52
Total outflow	4350	3200	4052
Ending cash balance	-3200	-2400	1598

You may be asked these questions about this chart:

What is the basis for your assumptions that were used to calculate these numbers?

How accurate do you think these numbers are?

Do they represent the 'worst case' the 'best case' or the probable (50%) case?

How will you pay us back if these numbers do not come true?

What exactly are the risks that these numbers will not be realized?

How much control do you have over these risks?

Remember: Most businesses that fail, do so because they run out of cash!

When using a chart of numbers or a graph in this book (or in a presentation) the question always comes "where do these numbers come from?" "How did you get them?"

These numbers do not represent an actual situation. They are for example only. When putting together your situation, you will develop first year numbers from experience in some cases. In other cases, you may have no experience upon which to base numbers at all. The only way to get the right numbers is by forming a small team, and finding out what the labor rates, the benefits, the costs of electricity, water, rental, bank loan interests, and all the other elements of cost. The list of costs must be thorough! List and estimate every cost possible, and know which are fixed and which are variable. Make up a cost of operations table like the one shown.

Fixed costs are those which you cannot change. No matter how much business you have, these costs stay "fixed". Examples of fixed costs are space rental, insurance, bank loan interests, operating labor, salaries, taxes, etc

Examples of variable costs are those which rise and fall directly with the amount of production or the number of clients your business has.

If your revenues (income generated by selling products or services, drops by half, you may have to cut salaries and operating wages. But normally, these are mostly fixed costs. Raw materials used to meet your business needs are all variable. This varies greatly with what your business does. If your business manufactures corn oil, raw materials will be a large part of your total cost.

Corn to corn oil

If your business is counseling and giving out advice, your raw material cost will be very small. Your costs would be much more variable, than fixed. If your costs are fixed and your business goes badly, or moves slowly, you will have difficulty in getting away from debt. In the operating cost chart on the next page, separate the fixed costs from the variable.

Operating Cost Estimating

The cost of operating your business must be carefully estimated. This is an example of how to make a detailed estimate for your business. It will not be exactly what yours is, but we use it as an example. Dollars/month during the first full year of operation. As stated before, using consistent units Is essential. Adding lb/mo and $/kg makes no sense at all. Adding capital expense to operating expense makes no sense either. Adding one time costs to monthly costs is also meaningless, but I have seen people do that. Apples + oranges= ??

Cost Item	Jan	Feb	Mar	Apr	May	Jun
Labor hourly	1000	1000	1000	1000	1000	1000
Hrly Benefits	50	50	50	50	50	50
Salaries	300	300	300	300	300	300
Sal Benefits	25	25	25	25	25	25
Your salary	300	300	300	300	300	300
Raw material	1200	1500	1600	1100	1200	1300
Packaging	100	130	140	105	100	135
Utilities(1)	100	110	120	125	125	129
Oper supp	50	75	60	65	70	50
Maint supp	10	14	17	18	19	21
Building rent	50	50	50	50	50	50
Loan Intr	15	15	15	15	15	15
Govt Taxes						400
Freight costs	10	12	15	10	17	16
Office cst (2)	2	5	3	4	5	6
Trash	1	1	1	1	1	1
Admin costs	2	2	2	2	2	2
Advertising	2	2	15	2	2	2
Sales costs	3	3	3	3	3	3
Research	0	0	15	15	0	0
All others	3	4	5	2	13	2
Equip rental	4	0	5	6	7	3
Total $/mo	3227	3598	3741	3198	3234	3809

Cost Item	Jul	Aug	Sept	Oct	Nov	Dec	Year
Labor hourly	1000	1000	1000	1000	1000	1000	12000
Hrly Benefits	50	50	50	50	50	50	600
Salaries	300	300	300	300	300	300	3600
Sal Benefits	25	25	25	25	25	25	300
Your salary	300	300	300	300	300	300	3600
Raw material	1700	1300	1200	1500	1500	1200	16300
Packaging	150	135	100	130	130	100	1455
Utilities(1)	132	125	115	110	100	95	1386
Oper supplies	60	50	55	65	75	80	755
Maint supplies	20	19	18	15	15	15	201
Building rent	50	50	50	50	50	50	600
Loan Intr	15	15	15	15	15	15	180
Govt Taxes							400
Freight costs	19	14	14	16	16	17	176
Office cst (2)	1	2	3	5	5	10	51
Trash removal	1	1	1	1	1	1	12
Admin costs	2	2	2	2	2	2	24

Advertising	2	10	2	2	2	2	45
Sales costs	3	3	3	3	3	3	36
Research	0	0	0	25	0	0	55
All others	3	1	6	8	2	5	54
Equip rentals	9	2	0	4	2	0	42
Total $/mo	3842	3404	3259	3626	3578	3270	41786

(1) Gas, electric, water, sewer usage

(2) Telephone, fax, computer, paper, all other office supplies

This may seem like an overly detailed exercise, but it is very worthwhile and it will force you to think about your cash position and variations in your cost by times of the year. When the lender shows interest in your proposal, you will have a better chance of being loaned capital if you can show a more careful analysis such as this. Also, thinking about how your business will be on a month to month basis, enables you to more realistically visualize your costs and how predictable they are, than trying to estimate your costs one year at a time.

Lines of Credit, Accounts Receivable/Accounts Payable

If you closely observe the cash flow and monthly cost projections in the tables above, it becomes obvious that getting set up for cash to start your business involves more than the initial expenditures for capital investment, startup cost and working capital. You will hire people even before revenues come in. You will also have to pay rent, pay for utilities and many other things prior to making any money. This may go on for months or even years. All during that time, you will need operating cash. Therefore you will need lines of credit to keep your business supported. In any discussion with the lender, no matter who they are, the lines of credit need to be understood and arranged.

There is a problem with the "Line of Credit" idea. Such an arrangement makes it too easy to keep borrowing, forever renewing your line of credit. This means forever paying back your debt plus interest. The sooner you can get away from this habit, the better. Do not substitute poor financial management and supporting that with credit loans, paying too much for rent (if you do that in the first place), going into too much debt overall, and not knowing the numbers enough and being surprised to find out you are in trouble financially already. Always know where you are financially! Continuing a line of credit would be a lenders dream come true! But it may ruin you. Lines of credit are meant to be short term, then stopped. You can hang yourself with lines of credit. Develop a strong habit of paying off debt quickly

Your most useful financial plan is a cash flow projection for <u>every month of the first three years</u>. You have an example above. This plan will need to account for all of the sources of income and expenses that are specific to your business, and when those sources of income or expenses occur. You will also want to account for any start-up capital and when that capital is raised.

How does one make projections in the financial plan that are reasonable and not unrealistic? Remember, in your sales plan you made monthly product sales projections that fit three scenarios. Your financial plan should evaluate all three of these scenarios and choose the projections that you feel most comfortable with. Or, if you want to be more precise, make two financial plans, one using the expected case projections, and one using the worst-case projections. Your end result will only be as good as the accuracy of your projections.

The major elements of income (inflow) in any business that may be included in your projection are:

- Sales of products/services
- Capital raised
- Donations
- Loan income
- Accounts Receivable and Accounts Payable

Just as your body needs blood in it to survive, your business needs cash in it to survive. Your business will die without a supply of cash. If you manage your business well, then the amount of money that you owe will always be less than the money owed to you. Preferably, your business can be done on a cash only basis. When you need supplies or need to pay the employees or the electric power bill or the rent, you have cash on hand to pay it, and not have to go back to the bank for this "line of credit" that is discussed above. A line of credit should be a last resort. Accounts payable is the money that you owe to pay your bills. Most of them you can plan on from month to month. When these bills come due, you can access cash from your business, and pay them.

Accounts receivable is the money that your customers owe you. If you run your business based on credit given to people who need your product but cannot pay you right away…then you need clear agreements, IOU's with penalties for failure to pay, contracts, to make it clear what is owed and when it is due. You will need a system to keep track of who owes your business money.

Always manage your business in a way that accounts receivable exceeds accounts payable. This may mean getting your money with an agreed upon payment schedule. Best of all is to deal only in cash from customers who buy from you. One of the biggest problems in the world of business today is non-payment of money owed to the business.

Words of Wisdom

Take the time to learn from the mistakes and successes of others. Always ask and then keep a record of what you learn.

"Everything should be made as simple as possible, but not simpler" A. Einstein

Honor God with a portion of your company profits, declaring that He is the true owner, the CEO of your company. Pray without ceasing for His wisdom.

Draw 2 or 3 neat diagrams showing what the layout and elevation view of your business will look like. A picture conveys much better understanding to the reader of what you propose. It also helps you decide how people will be allocated and the way they will work. These are "working diagrams".

In each element of the business plan, you need to decide how much risk you are willing to take. Can you really operate within the wide 10%-90% window, in every way? What is your tolerance for risk?

Develop your core values and stick to them. Examples might be core values such as:

- The customer is always right
- Safety first
- Equal treatment and opportunity for all employees
- We will always have the best quality
- Zero defects
- High ethical standards and integrity
- We'll meet or beat any price
- God is my senior partner. He will never fail you!

A clever business person is like a clever card player: "You have to know when to hold them, and when to fold them; when to walk away and when to run." There is a time to spend, and a time not to spend. What happens If we do NOT spend right now?

Spending money is a decision about choices. Always ask the question "Must we spend money on this"? Always consider that there are three choices; yes, no, or 'yes but later'. Often, the latter is the best choice.

"Follow the money" is always good advice. Be sure, however, that the flow of money is always going to be there, and not divert or dry up entirely. Are you located in a place in which you can sell your goods? Can customers easily find you? Are you in a market in which there is money being spent, now and in the future? If not, get out.

Locate well. A friend who operates 2 Chick-Fil-A stores tells me that success depends on four factors: location, location, location, location!

The Charcoal Pit restaurant in Wilmington, Delaware is one of my favorites because it takes me back to boyhood days, with the ambience of the '50's. It was located on a major, two lane highway in 1956 and offered hamburgers and milk shakes. At the time, there was no competition around, and it became very popular.

Fast forward to today, in 2019; the restaurant still looks the same, and the owners have changed many times, but hardly any money has been spent on improvements. It has become surrounded by competitors of all kinds. The highway has become a four lane instead of a two lane. It is almost hidden from view because of all the buildings next to it. Yet, it continues to be crowded at lunch and dinner times. When the management is asked why it is still so popular after all these years, they shrug their shoulders and answer "we keep our quality the same, and keep our staff happy...no one ever quits! Every customer who comes in knows they will be well treated and leave satisfied by good quality at good cost. That is why we have been here for 63 years!!"

Mt. Everest
Nepal

29,028 feet
8,848 meters

Consider Mount Everest: You'll never start at the top
Points to think about:

- You don't just decide one day to go climb it. You have to prepare yourself physically, mentally, financially and emotionally.
- You have to go through the training, make sacrifices, set aside other goals to achieve this one, invest your resources
- You need to surround yourself with a good team whom you trust.
- You will certainly need persistence, patience, perseverance, determination.
- "Pain is temporary, quitting lasts forever." Lance Armstrong
- Base camp 1   (6100 m) adjust to the altitude
- Base camp 2   (7300 m) advanced elevation
- Base camp 3   (8000 m) need lots of experience
- Base camp 4   (8600 m) you are now only two days away from the top at 8800m.
- Your time at the summit is brief! Time to start planning to turn it over to someone else. Do you have a plan for getting down?
- Success: Reaching the top and coming back safely! Success is hearing the Lord saying to you "well done, good and faithful servant". Don't forget who made the mountain! It's not yours, it's

His. Don't forget who made your business! Thank Him even on days when you don't feel very successful.

Exercises

You are a partner of a business in which you have already done a feasibility study, decided what business you will engage in, and have taken part in the types of analyses shown above. Discuss as a group the following three case studies, answering these questions for each:

"Is this going to be a successful business?"
"What was the problem?"
"What is the solution?"
"What should the owners do now?"

Case A – Recycled bottles

Plastic bottle waste is a growing problem as litter along the streets and highways. We have decided that such bottles, being made of a high grade of polyester and used for water and soft drinks, are valuable, and recoverable. Up until now, getting them collected has been hard to achieve but recently, the government has imposed a deposit on them such that all bottles come back to where they were purchased and money is refunded to the buyer. We decided that it was feasible to partner with large stores to take the bottles off their hands, and recycle them. We get a large supply of plastic bottles in that manner and the stores are very happy to have us take them away. Law prohibits their reuse for more beverages. We will supplement this supply by having individuals collect bottles and bring them to our recycle center, and be reimbursed a small amount for them. We have determined that our capital investment will be about $900,000 US and that we will need about 50 people to operate this place on a 5 day/week, 24 hour/day schedule. According to the business plan, the payback on the investment, borrowed from the bank, will be about 5 years. The price of the recycled plastic was set at $0.68 /lb. versus the market price for virgin plastic being at

$0.97/lb. and the cost to operate was determined to be about $0.45/lb. total for all materials, freight, loan repayment, packaging and operations. Technical feasibility was thought to be good, in separating the polyester plastic from all the other things in the mix of materials delivered (paper, metals, other).

The plant began on schedule, once the investment in equipment was made and all was properly installed, on budget, on time, safely. An opening ceremony was held, including government officials, who admired what such a plant would do for the environment and job creation. Initially, the product was of good quality and customers were placing orders for it. A good job of marketing had been done, apparently.

In four years, the enterprise went into bankruptcy because people were no longer interested in paying about $0.70 / lb. for this product when they could get "virgin" plastic of higher purity for the same price. The price of oil, from which virgin product is derived, had dropped significantly since the beginning, and that is what dictated its price.

Problem

What was the problem here? Failure to anticipate what could happen if the price of oil, the competitive raw material, changed in the wrong direction. We all know that the price of oil is cyclical, but how long are the cycles? Can our business hold out against a sustained low competitive price?

Solution

A properly done 10-50-90 analysis of this might have steered the partners in a different direction. While the project seemed feasible in many ways, they should have considered who the competition was and what little control they would have over it.

Case B – Coffee Shop

A person was very interested in starting a coffee shop in Nanjing, PRC. This city of 8 million abounds in universities (32) and college students (nearly one million), and with a growing affluence, and some interest in western style living, this city seemed like a good place to operate an American style coffee shop. Students are known to enjoy congregating in such places and talking, while eating and drinking. A feasibility study resulted in "full steam ahead" decision to make an investment and do this. The partners had done a lot of homework by finding out how many coffee shops already existed in Nanjing, and some had even gotten jobs in other coffee shops to see how they 'really worked'. They found that few people can own property in such a place, however, so they searched for a place to rent. They found one, well located close to some universities. The investment of about $100,000 US was made in the necessary equipment, and starting inventory of necessary ingredients, and they were 'open for business'. The partners pooled their own money for the investment, and the profit margins gave them the assurance that they would see a return on their investment in about 10 years. They saw business starting slowly, and as they became better known, and spread by word of mouth, it was expected to grow. Meanwhile, they knew where to obtain supplies at reliable prices, and so the supply chain of the many ingredients was well thought through. Yet, in the second year of their operation, they came into such problems that they went out of business. With a good business plan in place, so well considered it seemed, what could have happened?

Problem

Contracts in China tend to be by word of mouth and when the landlord decides to either increase the rental price or ask someone to leave, there is little that can be done about it. In this case, the landlord decided to force the coffee shop out in order to make way for his son to come in to use the same space for other purposes. He did this by simply doubling the rent without warning. This forced a well-established coffee shop to close down and move, risking loss of equipment, loss of some of the investment as well as being out of business for some time and having to find a whole new clientele.

Solution

The risk portion of the business plan needed to have been studied more, and the investors more alerted that such a thing could happen. This problem was brought about by insufficient dialog with the landlord ahead of time, and insufficient maintenance of guanxi, or relationship development. Perhaps the landlord should have become a silent partner in the business. Do you know your partners well? Did you expect the unexpected in your plans?

Case C – Flowers

Valik is a pastor in Ukraine. He and his wife have a small but growing church along a busy highway, near their house. He wanted to be more than just the pastor of a church, but the pastor of the whole village. Most people know gardening very well, and the land is supremely fertile, the black soil able to grow almost anything. During the last ten years, Ukraine has emerged into a country in which some of the population has disposable income and can spend some money on things beyond basic needs. For example, a segment of the population can build homes and grow flowers and shrubs. Valik decided to open up a garden center in front of their home on the busy highway. He buys flowers and shrubs and other lawn decorations, and sells them to people who pass by and see their sign (Valik and Natasha Garden Center). His business plan consisted of asking many people for advice and taking it to heart. He was advised to start small and work up, and to not promise more than he could deliver. He hired his mother and mother in law to tend the store, to welcome customers and show them around, and even gave them power to negotiate on price. His six children are soon old enough to help too. In addition, he hires about 20 people from his village who are not church members to tend the gardens. These are jobs that didn't exist in that village before. He has added something which is very unusual in the Soviet system in which he grew up: customer service. He will deliver ornamental trees and shrubs for free. He will also guide customers on how best to plant them and keep them healthy. Word is spreading that he is a fair business man, with Christian integrity and will do as he promised. If a customer does not like what he purchased, he can have his money back without questions (very unusual in that part of the world).

Valik has even built an outdoor toilet and shower facility at the garden center, and it is open to anyone from town or a customer. It's the only such facility in a town of 5000 people.

Question

What is Valik doing right? He started small and worked up. He entered into a business he knows a lot about. He had a minimal investment to begin with. He uses the natural resources where he lives to his advantage. He sees an emerging market and is even thinking about exportation by the truckload to EU countries. He gives God all the glory and honor in the conduct of the business. He involves local people who have never heard of Christ's love to help him.

What could have gone wrong?

Key learnings

- We learn that when we put God first in our business, that He will bless it in ways we cannot imagine.
- What would you do differently?

Case D - Colombian Restaurant

Carlos Melendez and his wife and two girls moved to the USA from Bogota, Colombia to find work and make a new life. Carlos had been an accomplished chef in his native Colombia, and after working at whatever became available in the US, he decided to open an authentic Colombian restaurant. After all, in the entire city, there was no such thing as a Colombian restaurant, and the delicious foods of his homeland were not available. He worked for another two years to gather the capital to build the restaurant, he surveyed the area to locate well, and did some advertising among friends and neighbors. He located near some office buildings and planned to sell empanadas to office workers in much the same way that people might order a pizza delivered, as an adjunct to his restaurant. When it came time to order the kitchen equipment, he took the advice of his parents back home, and ordered the best ovens and accessories directly from Colombia for the place in order to cook 'comida autentica' (authentic food).

This cost a lot more money that he had estimated, and the import duties on such equipment doubled the cost again! But having food cooked in the original way seemed to be worth it. The father and mother came to the US to see their son's work, and immediately ordered changes be made to many parts of the restaurant, all of which cost more money. They were anxious then to open for business as quickly as possible, so as to begin recouping some of the money they spent. Even though the place was not quite complete, they opened and started to receive customers.

Within a year, the doors closed. The parents returned to Colombia in disgust with their son for shaming them back home. Carlos was left with a lot of debt and no restaurant. Why did it fail?

Problem

When customers came to the establishment, they thought of it as just another good Tex-Mex place in town, but recognized almost nothing on the menu. Upon ordering, they seemed to wait forever to get their order, and sometimes would just get up and walk out. Those who did order and get food, liked it, but thought it was too expensive and not worth the cost or the long wait. People began to say to others that this was not one of the better places to eat.

Solution

This was the typical case of the clash of two cultures. Colombians hold their cuisine in high regard (and rightfully so), but no one in this area desired it or would pay 'extra' for it. The food had simply not been sold to the public very well as something to desire. In American culture, people tend to eat earlier in the evening, and as more of a necessity, than a 'dining event'. A successful restaurant in America seeks 'table turnover', with many people coming in, ordering, eating, paying, leaving and being replaced by more people. In Colombia, people eat later and occupy the table for the whole evening. Each dish is cooked to order in Colombia, and therefore takes time. In America, people will not wait for the kitchen to turn on the stove and get ready to cook the meal. The solution then would have been to understand the new culture better and not just assume that the old ways will be readily adopted by the new culture. It is also a lesson in allowing family members who have no financial vested interest in the business to have the power to make important decisions. If they have capital in the business, make them partners. If they don't, then it is right to tell them to "get out of the kitchen!"

Another exercise which is very helpful is called the "Failure Mode and Effect" analysis. Ask a trusted group of advisors, friends, partners, etc. to spend some time with you, examining your business idea, both at the planning stages and then later, as the business develops. The main idea is to ask these key questions, at each step of your business process:

At each step, what could fail? Supply chain? Safety? Product quality? Sales team? Where is the "weak link" in the chain?

If it did fail, what could be the result?

If the probability of failure is significant, and the effect is significant, then what can be done ahead of time to prevent failure? Must we change our methods, or build in a backup plan, or make some other provisions to protect our business from such an event? How much will such protection cost and how will we finance it?

Form small groups of 4 or 5 people if this study is being done in a class setting.

- Choose any one of the examples given above.
- Spend the necessary time to agree on the answers to these questions:
- What could have failed, or why did it fail?
- Who is responsible for the failure
- What should have been done to prevent that failure?
- Prioritize the failures by most critical to least critical

Exit Strategy

Every business plan needs an exit strategy. What will you do if your business meets unexpected difficulties and it is necessary to stop the business?

The Mango Berry example

Exit strategy and tough decisions-
The Mango Berry example

Mango Berry was the name of a small store which sold ice cream in a small shopping mall in Wilmington, Delaware, USA. This store stands beside many other stores, mòst of which have been there for 30 years or more. Mango Berry had been in operation for only 2 years and then it failed. The financials and morale of the store declined every month. They opened early and closed late, just to attract as many customers as possible. The place was spotless. The Board of Health would have given them an "A+" grade. Here are some of the facts about this business:

The couple who own it also operate it, and borrowed $100,000 to set up the store.

The gross sales are $91,000 per year

The rental on the store area is $31,200 per year. That, plus all of the other expenses in ingredients, electricity, taxes, etc exceed $91,000 per year!

While they offer the best price in town, and also have the most healthy food, very few people seem to want it

This store is also very clean and orderly, impressive when a customer first walks in the door

The couple who own and operate it begin work at 900 in the morning, and close at 2200 at night, 7 days a week

They have no idea how to market their store or product, and few people have even heard about it. They offer no incentives to come in and buy their product, such as coupons, or "buy one, get one free", or "here is a small cup, take a free taste of any flavor you like!" In the part of the world where they come from, you give NOTHING away for "free".

Another similar store across town is not as clean, and offers small cups for free samples that the customer can pour at their own discretion. The attendants behind the counter are young, pretty girls. The couple at Mango Berry, by contrast, are quite elderly, grumpy and don't have a good command of English.

The couple now wants to just sell the store and go away from the business, very discouraged, admitting failure, and deeply in debt. Their adult children are furious with them for failing. They will gladly sell the business for $30,000 to anyone. The sooner, the better!

Given these facts and observations, what would you suggest the couple do now? Why do you think they are having trouble? What would you suggest could be done, other than sell it? Should they stop losing money now and sell it, the sooner, the better? Write your thoughts on the space below.

If such misfortune happens to your business, you must have a plan already in hand, for cutting your losses and getting out. What is your exit strategy?

Non-Governmental Organizations (NGO's)

Perhaps profit is not your motive for setting up a business. There are more than 50000 NGO's in the world today and their goal is to set up a business which doesn't make a profit, but earns enough money to support itself and employ people to help others. It is a primarily humanitarian effort. Any profit which is made is put back into the effort to help more people in desperate need. These needs can include better drinking water supply, climate improvement, curbing hunger, improving health, reducing poverty, strengthening social justice, education and many other world needs. Neither the government nor the military take part in an NGO, except for the initial approvals. Those who set up an NGO usually work through the local community because it is for that community's benefit. Many NGO's depend on volunteers to do the work. Let's take one example: Partners in Health takes a holistic approach to improving the health of many people in impoverished areas of the world, providing medicines and teaching hygiene and home health care. There is no profit. The basic steps described in this book apply to starting an NGO as well. I believe a place to begin your research is the United Nations Development Program. www.undp.org

Chapter 5 Marketing and Sales Plan

Subject:	Development of Marketing and Sales Plans
Lesson Objectives:	1. How to use a marketing plan effectively
	2. How to develop your specific marketing plan
	3. How to develop your company's sales strategy
	4. Understand the difference between marketing and sales
	5. How to prepare and use a budget
	6. Retail versus wholesale
Books recommended	"The Everything Business Plan Book", Ramsey and Windhaus
	"EntreLeadership", Dave Ramsey
	"The Innovator's Dilemma", Dr. Clayton Christensen

Introduction

Marketing and sales are often hard to distinguish. Smaller organizations usually combine them. The larger the organization, the more the two are regarded as separate functions. Here is a simple definition:

Marketing's purpose is to understand the needs of the customers, develop new products, advertise to raise public awareness of your products or services, and to increase interest in your company and what you do. Marketing answers the question: where should we go with our products?

Sales' purpose is to apply all of marketing's findings and directly interact with customers who will exchange your products and services for money. Sales answers the question: how can we keep our customers loyal to our company, meet their needs and bring money into our accounts? Sales is the public "face" of our company. We need to develop a good Marketing and Sales Plan.

- The elements of a marketing plan
- When to put together a marketing plan?
- Who should be involved in building the marketing plan?
- Marketing plan contents
- What happens if you do not have a marketing plan?
- How should you use a marketing plan?
- How should you revisit your marketing plan, and revise it as needed?

Marketing Plan

Where to start. You have finished your feasibility study and identified which product and/or service you will provide as a business. You are in the midst of writing your business plan, and need to decide just how you will quantify your market, and then sell the products. Reviewing the questions above:

A. When to do your marketing plan: now

B. Who should be involved? You and a group of people who you can trust to answer some key issues by thorough study, and assess risk. A committee of 3 or 4 is good, and they could be people you hire from the outside who have no other vested interest in your company. You, the entrepreneur or owner, need to be on the committee. You set the boundaries for what is to be studied and how much time the committee has to come back with answers.

Key Questions answered for your "product"

What are the industry trends? Look at the past 5 years, and see how rapidly the market has grown. Make a 10-50-90 prediction of how you believe the sales of this product will grow in the next 5 years. Just to review the definitions:

90 % represents the worst-case scenario. Surely, these goals can be reached with 90% certainty. But are they good enough to keep you in business?

50% represents the average scenario; the most likely case, with a 50% chance of being better and a 50% chance of being worse

10% represents the best-case scenario. Higher numbers but with uncertainty attached. If you achieve these, are you able to meet the demands? Your estimates may look like this: (also refer to the palm oil example given earlier)

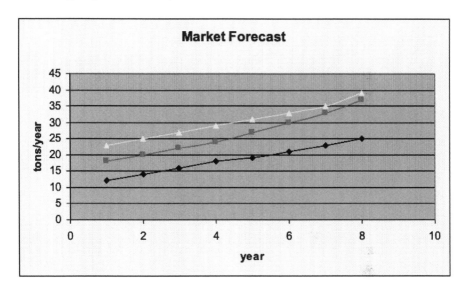

Which line represents which case? Which is the 10%, which the 50% and which is the 90%?

Pricing

Next, do the same type of analysis for the pricing of the product. How has the pricing for products similar to yours changed in the past 5 years, and why have they changed? Again, refer back to the palm oil example.

Industry trends

Describe this industry as to whether or not it is....

- Growing and expanding
- Stagnant or staying flat, or stable or "mature"
- Falling or declining due to competition or other factors
- Seasonality
- How does this market rise and fall depending on the time of the year?
- Does this market depend greatly on holidays?
- How sensitive is this market to economic cycles, such as clothing fashions, tastes, inflation, unemployment, etc.?

Technological changes

Is a new technology likely to come along and change what you propose to offer? What are the chances for 'disruptive technology' closing out the need for your business?

Regulations and Certification

Have you gone to the local governments and made certain that your plans will not be stopped by some regulation. Have you met all government requirements? You may need your business plan as a reference in case tough questions are asked.

Supply and Distribution Channels

What plans have you made to keep your business supplied and your products stored once they are made and then distributed safely? This will represent working capital money that you might not have anticipated.

Your Target Market

How would you describe your customers? Can you identify them by name, know where they are located, quantify them, describe them demographically, know if they can actually pay you for what you sell them? Your target market must be:

- Describable geographically
- Definable
- Sizable and quantifiable
- Reachable
- Stable

Branding

Do you have a recognizable brand name? Are you competing against a well-recognized brand name? Is your brand name easy to say and remember? Once you get a good brand name, never 'throw it away'! Can you imagine McDonald's discarding the golden M and replacing it with something else? Can you imagine KFC throwing away the caricature of Colonel Sanders?

The value of a good brand

The Competition

- Who are your competitors? Learn as much as possible about them.

- How aggressive are your competitors? Will they drop their price the moment you start your business?

True story: J D Rockefeller began shipping crude oil from his oil fields in Ohio to his refineries in New Jersey, by rail. A competitor decided to build a pipeline from their oil fields to New Jersey, and deliver oil to the refineries at a lower price than Rockefeller could. He waited for them to complete the pipeline (at great cost). Once completed, the oil started to flow. Rockefeller dropped the price of his oil and his kerosene. The new competitors could not match his lower price without losing money. They wanted to maintain the higher price in order to recoup their recent debt in the pipeline. Finally they were forced to sell the pipeline and Rockefeller bought it at a small fraction of what they had put into it. Then he began to put the pipeline to his own use, and that forced the railroad to drop their shipping price. Now in control, Rockefeller raised the price to where it had been, and his profits increased greatly. (this is now illegal behavior in the US but in many countries, it is not).

Are you ready for tough competition?

Think about what you would do.

What could have gone wrong here?

Customer Perception

What will the customer think of you and your product and your company?

If they feel cheated or charged too much, or that they waited too long, they will go somewhere else the next time. Furthermore, if they feel that they simply are not getting their money's worth, they will spread the word that you are not a good person or place to do business with. The end result will be that you will go out of business and carry a bad reputation with you.

Scripture mentions honesty with weights and measures quite frequently. Examples are found in Proverbs 11:1, 20:10 and

Leviticus 19:35-36, explaining that cheating is displeasing to God and consequences result. The bad behavior of the tax collectors, in unfairly charging more than they should have, is a social injustice.

If the customer feels, however, that they have been treated fairly, and gotten their money's worth, and liked their first experience with you and your business, they will come back, and bring others with them. Your good reputation will expand throughout the community and your business will grow and prosper. Train each of your employees to treat customers well.

True story: A man and his wife wanted to build a house, and hired a contractor to do the work. They agreed on the plans, and many details. Both were excited about their new, future house. The price agreed upon was fixed and the contract was signed. The start date was also agreed upon. Indeed, the work began on time. However, the contractor constantly complained that his workers did not show up for work, and the completion date kept getting pushed back more and more. By the time the house was ready to move into, many months had passed by, and the couple had to pay much more rent than they had planned. When they finally moved into the new house, there was evidence right away that the quality of the house was not good. The floors moved when people walked across them! The doors did not fit or close properly, and air flowed through closed windows. Lights in some areas were dim, and when more than one appliance was plugged into electrical sockets, the whole house went dark because a circuit couldn't carry the load.

Further inspection showed that the contractor had accepted other jobs at the same time, and had redeployed his workers to those instead of finishing the job he had agreed to do. Also, he "saved money" for himself by "cutting corners", or putting in cheaper materials of construction.

1. Where were the mistakes made?
2. What should have been done to avoid such mistakes?

3. How will that building contractor market his work and expertise in the future?
4. What is the perception of his customers from this point forward?

Customer treatment

Emmanuel and the Car Repair

Emmanuel and I planned our itinerary to give several seminars about Christian business in a route from south to north in Cote d'Ivoire, beginning in Abidjan. To do this, he had planned to use his own automobile. He first had to take it to his trusted mechanic for a routine oil change. "This shouldn't take long", he assured me with confidence. The owner of the shop gave the assignment to a new employee, who placed the car on the lift, and proceeded to take off the oil filter from under the engine block. In doing so, he stripped the threads from the place where the oil filter screws into the block, destroying it for a replacement filter. This would not be easy or quick to correct! At first, the owner told us to come back in 3 days and he would have fixed the problem. But we had conferences arranged and could not do that. Next he told us where to go to rent a car for the week. By now, delay was building up and the situation did not look very good. Finally, the owner handed the keys to his Mercedes to Emmanuel and told him to take good care of his car, and come back in a week, and he would have his car repaired. In a nicely air-conditioned vehicle, we were on our way and met all of our appointments. At the end of the week, Emmanuel's car was as good as new.

Our impression of the owner could not have been higher! Will we keep coming back? Yes. Will we spread the word about this man's efforts to take good care of his customers? Of course, gladly.

YOUR GOOD REPUTATION IN BUSINESS IS LIKE GOLD! TREASURE IT! BUILD IT! ENLIST ALL OF YOUR EMPLOYEES TO HELP YOU DO THAT.

Marketing plan example

This is an example of an executive summary for a marketing plan for a startup company. The company will sell Internet services to the general public.

MARKETING PLAN SUMMARY for CAPITAL CITY CAFÉ

This summary presents a five-year plan for establishing "The Capital City Internet Café and Lounge" starting in November, 2019. Research has shown that many university students like to come together to discuss issues of the day and to study in a clean, safe environment. Many of them do not have reliable computers, or ways to do research on the Internet. We have interviewed many students and found that there is a market for a place which not only offers Internet services, but a place to meet and drink tea and coffee, and socialize. We propose to establish an internet café and lounge near the university campus, attract students, and offer reliable services which work all the time. We will invest in space, new computer equipment, printers, faxes, and a coffee bar with comfortable furniture, all at a cost of $20,000. We will publicize our place of business on a website, which will cost an additional $1,000 to develop. While there certainly are many competitors in the same city, our central location, and our combination of computer services and a coffee lounge, will attract many students and business people as well. We plan to promote our business by offering a one-year membership in a way that gives members a discount, and by extending their membership for one free month for each new person who becomes a member. We plan to earn a reputation in the city for fair prices, good services and a clean, safe environment in which to spend valuable time. Finally, we anticipate that our place of business will add 10 new jobs to the area which do not exist now. In five years, we expect that the business will have grown to the point, profitably, that we can develop two new such places within a 6 km radius of the first one.

Questions:

1. Why is your overall impression positive or negative?
2. What is missing from this description?
3. Do you believe that this business is sustainable, and why?
4. What downside risks are there?
5. How can such risks be mitigated?
6. Just how long ago was this marketing research carried out?

Assignment: Given the feasibility study we did recently, and choosing a business which appeals to you, write your own marketing plan.

Sales Plan and the budgeting process

A sales plan is different from a marketing plan in that it involves direct interaction with customers, service to them, and probably price negotiation. Selling involves educating the customer about your products, and convincing them that they have a need for it that they cannot do without. What are some important elements of your sales plan?

Know your product well and understand how it is priced. News travels fast. How you deal with one customer will quickly spread to others. How well did you meet their needs, how fair is your pricing, how good was your follow-up, how well does your product/service perform?

Be willing to set your own schedule aside and serve your customer.

When you have made a sale, be sure than you invoice the customer. Many business people never send an invoice! Therefore, they will have cash flow problems. You must be paid!

How will you take customer orders?
- By personal visits?
- On the phone?
- From the internet?
- Walk in customers?

How will you staff your sales force? That will depend on how you answer C above. It will also be determined by many other factors, such as the type of product you are selling, the size of your business, etc.

Have a clear method of documenting customer orders and then tracking them, to be sure that they are filled on time and accurately. When the customers have paid for the order, keep a book which records the customer name, what was sold, the amount for which it was sold and the date of the sale.

Scripture teaches us to tell the truth. It may not be what the customer wants to hear, but it needs to be the truth. Let your "yes" mean "yes" and your "no" mean "no" (Matthew 5:37). Many cultures have the habit of telling you what they "think" you want to hear.

When you are trying to sell your product, someone may give you a recommendation about a possible sale. You follow up on that recommendation, and it succeeds. Should you give some of the money from that sale to the person who gave you the recommendation, or not? The answer is up to you. I would say that it is a good idea to do that. You may consider it a "finder's fee" or simply a gift of gratitude. Perhaps you can write that gift off from your taxes as a cost of sales.

Have a customer complaint system in place, so that customers feel satisfied with your service and will come back (and bring friends).

Contracts for larger sales are important. Write them and sign them by both your business and the customer. The better they are written, the better they will serve the needs of both. Be aware that in some parts of the world, contracts are in force only until the customer finds a better offer. At that point, your contract goes in the wastebasket.

Sales forecasting is important as it is an essential part of your business plan, and needs to be kept before you all the time as you operate the business. It is the best way of monitoring how well you are doing month by month, year by year. Having a good sales forecast enables you to make changes to your business to either accommodate more sales than you expected, or to save money because sales are less than expected. Using the lady who makes garments as an example, here might be her sales forecast for the next year after she makes the investment in an embroidery machine:

SALES OF GARMENTS MADE IN 2014, in numbers of garments

Month	Jan	Feb	Mar	Apr	May	Jun
Shirts A	10	12	11	11	11	10
Shirts B	0	1	1	2	4	6
Total	10	13	12	13	15	16

Month	Jul	Aug	Sep	Oct	Nov	Dec	Year
Shirts A	12	11	10	12	10	12	132
Shirts B	9	10	10	12	11	13	79
Total	21	21	20	24	21	25	211

- Shirts A are those without embroidery,
- Shirts B are those with embroidery

During the year of making and selling shirts, what questions may come to her mind as she 'watches her sales'?

Should she be discouraged at the end of January? No

If she made her goal to have sold 100 of the A and 100 of the B by the end of 2014, should she be discouraged? No

Is it evident that having the ability to offer both A and B services, is helping the A business for which she is well known already? Yes, that could be.

Is there any evidence of seasonality in her business? Not really.

Given this first-year performance, in which she offered both A and B, what changes should she make in order to forecast for the next year?

Would any of these changes prompt her to be better equipped to handle that forecast?

For example: hire another person, repair Machine A, buy some spare parts for either Machines A or B, build some inventory in textiles and other supplies (buttons, embroidery, etc) so that she can offer better service and save money by buying in larger quantities and make her profit margin even better?

Exercises

Exercise 1

Given that the sales for 2014 are as shown above, and that shirts A sell for $10/each, and shirts B sell for $15 each, convert the sales forecast from numbers of shirts, to dollars forecast.

SALES OF GARMENTS MADE IN 2014, in dollars of sales

Month	Jan	Feb	Mar	Apr	May	Jun	Jul	Aug	Sep	Oct	Nov	Dec	Year
Shirt A													
Shirt B													
Total													

Using these two forecasts, create a forecast for the next five years, month by month, then year by year.

Exercise 2

Based on this information over the next five years, ask yourself the same questions as given in point 6 above, and list your answers on the next page. How would you prepare for this future? If you are really earnest, your forecasting should take the form of the 10-50-90 probabilities discussed in the previous examples. How would you apply this example to your business?

Budgeting for your business

The Sales forecast above is the basis for making up your budget. A budget is often made, then ignored. However, it is very helpful for planning what your business will need to prepare for hiring additional people, for making new capital investments, for perhaps moving your business location or establishing a second one.

Based on the sales forecast above and the corresponding equivalent forecast in dollars:

SALES OF GARMENTS MADE IN 2014, in numbers of garments

Month	Jan	Feb	Mar	Apr	Ma	Jun	Jul	Aug	Sep	Oct	Nov	Dec	Year
ShirtA	10	12	11	11	11	10	12	11	10	12	10	12	132
ShirtB	0	1	1	2	4	6	9	10	10	12	11	13	79
Total	10	13	12	13	15	16	21	21	20	24	21	25	211

- Shirts A are those without embroidery and sell for $10/each. Shirts B are those with embroidery and sell for $15/each.
- The cost to make shirt A is $8.50/shirt, and to make shirt B is $10/shirt. We are assuming for simplicity that all costs are variable.

SALES OF GARMENTS MADE IN 2014, in dollars of sales

Month	Jan	Feb	Mar	Apr	May	Jun	Jul	Aug	Sep	Oct	Nov	Dec	Year
ShirtA	100	120	110	110	110	100	120	110	100	120	100	120	1320
ShirtB	0	15	15	30	60	90	135	150	150	180	165	195	1185
Total	100	135	125	140	170	190	255	260	250	300	265	215	2505

Now calculate the revenue coming in each month based on this information.

EXPECTED COST PER MONTH IN 2014, in dollars

Month	Jan	Feb	Mar	Apr	May	Jun	Jul	Aug	Sep	Oct	Nov	Dec	Year
ShirtA	85	102	94	94	94	85	102	94	85	102	85	102	1124
ShirtB	0	10	10	20	40	60	90	100	100	120	110	130	790
Total	85	112	104	114	134	145	192	194	185	222	195	232	1914

- Do you have enough money each month to pay the bills in order to produce the garments?
- How much money should you have saved for unexpected expenses in the following months?
- How will you set aside enough money so that, when you have months in which sales are less, you can still pay the monthly bills?

In this example, each month brings in more revenue after the bills have been paid. This is often not the case, and you as the entrepreneur must be prepared for that.

Notice that the costs include the owner's salary. You have already been paid! The remaining revenue is considered company earnings, and that will be taxable income.

Remember: most businesses fail because they mismanage their money and have none left when there are low months.

Remember: many businesses do not manage money well because they do not separate company money from personal money. One of the elements of cost is <u>your own salary</u>!! You must pay yourself every month! When someone (often a family member) comes to you and says:

"You have a company and you have money. I have this 'need' and so I ask you to do a big favor for me. Please give me some money from your company (after all, it IS yours, isn't it?) and I will surely pay you back soon."

If you do that even ONE TIME, you are heading for failure in your company. That will begin a stream of people asking for money that will never end until you finally have no money left, and your business is gone! Here is the proper way to handle such requests, by answering:

"No, I can't do that, no matter who you are and no matter how great the need"

"This business does not belong to me; it belongs to God. I am His steward, taking care of it for Him"

"perhaps I can help you out of my personal money, but I cannot give you money from the business funds".

You must protect your business because it has been entrusted to you by God to flourish and give Him praise and glory and honor. Perhaps you feel badly that you cannot hand money to someone who asks for it.

But you must trust God, as said so well in Proverbs: "Trust in the Lord with all of your heart, and do not depend on your own understanding; in all your ways, depend on Him and He will make your paths straight."

If you keep your company funds separated clearly from your personal funds, and manage each of those well, you will be able to succeed. If you do not keep them separate, and do not manage each of them well, you will probably fail.

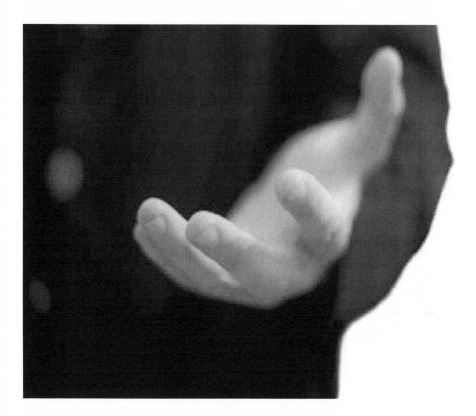

It is clear that this is very difficult to do in many cultures which have a "reciprocity" understanding; the idea that if I give you something, then you "owe me" when I need something. Think carefully how to circumvent that cultural habit.

This budget can be the basis upon which you decide to hire more people and for what tasks. For example, if the sales of embroidered shirts is going very well, you may consider hiring someone specifically for that task. Had you not kept good records of your sales, and did not know how much income was coming from the sales of embroidered shirts, you might not know who and when to hire someone.

My father was a self-employed businessman who sold large, refrigerated cases for supermarkets to use for frozen vegetables and meat. He went into a partnership with an exuberant fellow salesman. Upon the first sale of $100000, the partner took the profit from that first sale and held a big party for his large family. All his relatives were invited! Let's eat, drink and be merry!! My father was furious at how his partner squandered the profit from this hard-earned sale. It was the end of that partnership!! Be careful to vet all potential partners!

The numbers above need to be used to make a forecast of what your business future will be. They are your starting point. Add to these information which you have gathered by consulting with others, making observations, and by making any changes that you consider necessary which might affect the years to come. The lady who owns the shirt business in Cote d'Ivoire is actually doing very well, 7 years after our first consultation together. She and her daughter work well together as partners. Based on her first and second years, and understanding where her competition is and what their capabilities are, and knowing who will be repeat customers who have spread the word about her expertise, and that she treats all customers with respect as a Christian should, she can make the following forecast about her shirt business.

Year	1	2	3	4	5
Shirt A, shirts/year	132	144	144	144	144
Shirt B, shirts/year	79	90	120	144	144
Shirt C, shirts/year	0	0	10	30	50
New investment, $	500		500		
People needed	2	2	3	3	3

She is planning to reach maximum capacity with her two sewing machines by the end of year 2, and go back to the bank for another $500 loan to add a third sewing machine and a third person. What other things might she need? More space? Better supply chain? Should she be setting aside some money for the third machine so she doesn't have to go back to the bank? (YES)

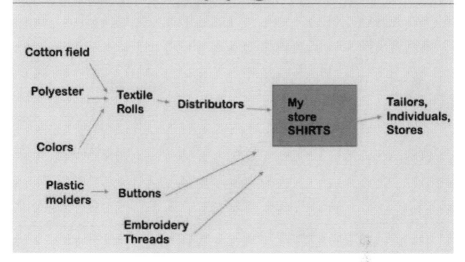

Shirt Supply Chain

Cotton field

Polyester → Textile Rolls → Distributors → My store SHIRTS → Tailors, Individuals, Stores

Colors

Plastic molders → Buttons

Embroidery Threads

Will one of her employees become a competitor once she trains them? (happens all the time!)

In general, most goods are sold either wholesale or retail. What's the difference?

Retail is familiar to everyone because when you go to a store and pay for something, you are shopping retail. To be a retail customer means to pay for the goods which includes a profit for the store or company who sold it to you. You deal directly with the store employees, and if you have to return the goods for credit or money back, you deal with that store. In some countries, that is commonly done; in others it is never done. The sales are final. The lady selling shirts in Africa is selling retail. Any profit from that sale is hers. If a shirt does not fit well, then adjustments can be made directly with her.

Another example is Valik, the pastor and businessman in Ukraine who sells ornamental plants and flowers, all of which he raises. His customers drive by his garden, stop and buy. Problems are handled directly through him. He wants to increase his customer base.

His brother-in-law, Cees, is five miles away and has many acres of ornamental trees of many categories. He doesn't sell one at a time, but in truckload quantities. His customers are not individuals, but large stores, who then sell to individuals. He has to sell larger volumes because his customers, the stores, have to make a profit too. His profit margin may be a little lower than Valik's on each plant, but his volume makes up for that. In summary:

Wholesale

- Wholesale means to sell in larger quantities but at lower margin
- Wholesale means to have much more in inventory at one time
- Wholesale means to pay more in shipping, taxes and insurance.
- Wholesale means to pay salesmen to represent you in the marketplace of fewer customers. If you lose one account, it is very significant to your business!
- Wholesale means to operate in a "make to inventory" mode, meaning in larger quantities and risking that what you produce is still in demand when it is ready to be shipped
- Wholesale means to carry a large working capital in unsold goods for a period of time. How much and how long depends on what you are selling.

Retail

- Retail means to sell at smaller quantities but at higher margin
- Retail means to have a smaller inventory at one time
- Retail means to pay less for shipping and taxes because you manufacture or grow your own product.
- Retail means having some employees who work for you directly and are the face of your business to your customers.

- Retail usually means operating in a "make to order" mode, getting what the customer needs when they need it.
- Retail usually means carrying a smaller inventory, and therefore less working capital tied up in unsold goods.
- Retail tends to have many more competitors who are trying to take a larger share of the total business.

One friend of mine who operates Haldas Meat Market says that he is constantly trying to "reinvent" himself; take out older items for sale, and bring in new ones before his competitors do. For example, at one time he had a "quality meat shop". But many people offer that now, and he offers a lunch truck which goes to businesses at lunch time when workers can take lunch break and get something fresh from the truck. He's known as "the man with the sauce", and everybody knows full well that John Eletheriou loves God.

Kohl's often locates their department stores (all retail) in strategic areas away from other stores. In order to get to the store, one must drive there and park the car. The stores are well stocked with clothing and jewelry items. Once you have gone into the store, there is no place else to go unless you return to your car and drive somewhere else. This is good psychology: why give the customer the option to walk next door to your competitor? This captures a segment of human behavior. "I'm here now, let's look around and when I see what I want, or something close to that, I'll buy it! "So the challenge is to draw customers in, knowing that once inside, they will get the business. Think of the convenience! "I get good quality, plenty of choices, in nice surroundings, and all at good prices and with helpful employees to guide me in finding my needs."

In addition, Kohl's gives customers up to a 30% discount for using their credit card. As long as that card is paid off promptly to avoid interest payments, it is well to use it. In so doing, the customer is eligible to receive "Kohl's Cash", a coupon entitling them to use it providing that the customer spends $50 or more. The customer feels like they have received fair deals and keeps coming back! Happy customers usually return!

Reminders of things often overlooked

1. You must pay yourself a salary

2. Retained earnings – you must have cash to operate your business, just as a car needs oil for the engine!

3. Cash flow reminds us to keep some cash on hand at all times. You can't run a business without cash.

4. Company money is NOT YOUR money ! (See Luke 11)(Psalm 24:1)

Chapter 6 Human Resources

Subject:	Human Resources-finding and hiring employees
Lesson Objectives:	1. Understand the principles of human resources 2. How and when to find and hire the right people for the job 3. How to keep the people you have hired and now depend on 4. Which organizational style is best for you?
Book recommendations	"E-Myth Revisited", by Michael Gerber "Leadership Coaching", by Tony Stoltzfus "Success God's Way", by Charles Stanley " Fierce Conversations", by Susan Scott

Introduction

You have completed the business plan and your partners have agreed to it. Like any business, it starts small, and grows. Do you plan to handle all of the business affairs yourself, or will you hire people to help you? Have you had a discussion with your partners about how many people it will take to operate the business, from the beginning and as it grows? That time has come!

Scriptural teaching which says ""Whoever can be trusted with little, can be trusted with much; and whoever is dishonest with little, will be dishonest with much." This tells us the importance of having trusted employees. Your company's reputation depends on it!

Earlier, I presented a personal experience in designing, building and staffing a plant here in the USA for recycling large volumes of polymer fiber waste. Several months before the startup of that plant, we put an advertisement for 'help wanted, 45 positions available', in the local newspaper. On the appointed day, a very bitterly cold

145

one at that, there were 2500 people answering the ad, lined up in cars, campers, trucks, some even standing in the cold. A partner and I interviewed many of them, to get the best 45. We were ready with full job descriptions, including answers to the inevitable questions, such as "what are the wages?", or "when do we start?" or "what kind of benefits are being offered?" or "is this an open shop or closed shop?" with respect to labor unions. Most of the applicants had been used to working union, and expected to come under similar organization. It was open shop.

The majority of the applicants were not well qualified based on the job description requested. Some did not tell the truth about their qualifications and while sounding good, had to be checked out. Others were clearly qualified, having had some prior experience. Choosing only 45 was a difficult task, but we did that. It was not easy telling late applicants "we are sorry, but our needs have been met already. We will keep your name on file and if we can use you, we will call you."

Several people, including me, were involved in operator and mechanic training. This small number were hired and put on the payroll right away, even though we' were months away from startup and production, and even more months away from seeing income flow back into the business. These were people who would be shift supervisors, and who would be instrumental in training the people who would work under them. These supervisors were flown to several of the equipment vendors who ran tests on the exact products we would be making, so they could see it, watch the fine points, gather information and take notes, develop their own expertise about what to do in case a problem occurred, about safety concerns, quality control, etc. I wanted them to become the 'experts' in the process, to "own it" and make it "their process". I did not want to be the only person knowing how to operate the plant, and the only one who would be called at midnight! I felt that it was critical for each person to take pride in the operation.

My experience in this was repeated 5 more times, in different parts of the country (USA) and in other parts of the world. Each time, I learned how to obtain the best people and instill in them a pride of "ownership" in their job performance. One objective was always to hire people whom I had high confidence in company loyalty. If the turnover rate was high, something needed to be changed to make people stay. Training is not cheap, and losing people can be disruptive to the business if not done well. I believe these practices would apply well to any business, anywhere in the world, regardless of culture.

It is a great source of pride to return to some of these plants and find people who have worked there for 35 years or more. Some I hired that cold day in January!

The elements of a plan to find, hire, fire and manage employees

The number, and the type of employees for your business will change with time and vary with the way your business grows. There is a very strong relationship between the success of your business and the type of people you have working in it. Your employees, beginning with yourself, are the 'public face' of your business and what the public knows about it will be determined to a large extent by the way those in your business treats them; financially, verbally, fairly, the quality of the workmanship and the service given.

The basic elements of this employee plan guideline will be:

- Assessing your company's needs
- Writing job descriptions (see page 115 for an example)
- How to find workers who will be productive
- How to interview workers and select the right ones
- How to manage compensation of workers
- How to manage worker benefits
- How to treat workers fairly and keep them
- How to manage your workforce when business is erratic and unpredictable
- How to fire employees when necessary

- Where to start

Remember that it is always easier to HIRE people than to FIRE them. Firing an employee is painful. Therefore, start with the minimum number of people and increase people only when you really need to. This chart illustrates how your business may look over a span of time.

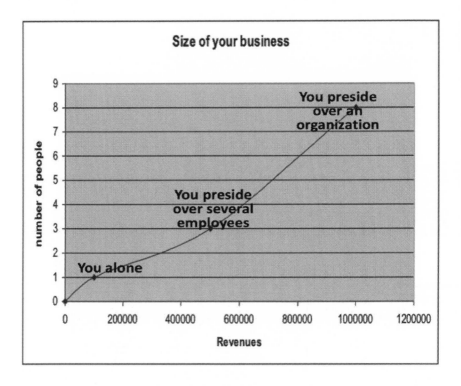

Your business may increase in number, or change in the types of expertise needed. In the introductory example, the needs grew from 45 to around 400 in both number and expertise. The process equipment become more complex and needed more specialized maintenance. The laboratory tests became more sophisticated and different people and/or more training was needed. Interface with the customers increased, and that required expertise which we didn't need at first, but grew with time. The chart below uses one simple measure of the need for more people: revenue. Covering the need for people is in fact more complicated than that and differs for any

148

business. We established a clear basis for promotion and related responsibilities. Throughout, maintaining a strong safety policy was implemented. We did not want anyone to be injured! And in 35 years, no one was!

This chart illustrates the growth of any company (hopefully). While numbers might be different, the idea is still the same. In the beginning you might be the only employee! This means that you will perform ALL the tasks, from production, to testing, to accounting, secretarial, sales, janitorial, planning; everything is your job. No job will be too great or too small. It doesn't matter where your 'strengths' or 'gifts' or talents lie; you do everything.

But above a certain level, you will need help. It is in this area where you need to ask yourself some honest questions. "What are my strengths and weaknesses, and what are my likes and dislikes? What am I really GOOD at, and where could I use some help?" "What do I have to do every day, but don't really enjoy it and don't even have time for it anymore?" Consider having someone you know, help you in this self-evaluation. At this level, more people are needed and this book will help you in identifying and hiring the right people. These are the people whom you will hopefully keep and train and rely upon as your company grows to be in charge of various parts of the task and to train others. At this level, you are learning how to manage others. Something you haven't done before because you have never had to!

At still a higher level, you must train managers how to manage. Your organization will now contain more than two levels of people involved in departments of your company. For example, your sales manager must manage salesmen, and your production manager must manage and train workers, etc. You will manage each of the managers. You should by this time, begin to think about who will replace you when you are out of town for long periods of time, or decide to retire.

In his classic book, "The E-Myth Revisited; why most small businesses don't work and what to do about it", Michael Gerber categorizes three types of business people

- Technicians...those who can't keep their hands away from the equipment and who insist on running everything. Always 'tinkering'. About 70% of the small businesses in operation are owned by tinkerers. They eventually fail.
- Managers...those who are in the office planning, charting, organizing, enforcing the rules. They find comfort in order. These people actually fear innovation! About 20% of the small businesses are owned by managers.
- Entrepreneurs...those who see opportunities and possibilities beyond the present confines, living in the future, as Gerber says. They live in a "what if..." world. They ask about change. They do not want to do the work of operators or managers. About 10% of the small businesses are owned by entrepreneurs.

With this as a framework, we shall now discuss the art of finding and hiring the right people, firing people when necessary and managing people with the right balance of objectives and skills.

Employee Management

Assessing your company's needs

At the beginning, during the business plan preparation, it was advised that you prepare a few drawings of your workplace, no matter what type of workplace it is. These drawings are useful for you to imagine 'where' people will work for you. Put 'people' on such a drawing. It might illustrate a Bed & Breakfast, a coffee shop, two sewing machines, a plastics factory or anything else. Please make a drawing. If you can't do it, have someone else do it. A picture is worth a thousand words indeed!

Next, think carefully about what each person will do at that point. As closely as possible, think about each part of their assigned task. Think about what skills these people will need. Should the people bring these skills with them, or can they learn on the job?

Next, ask yourself what your business would look like if you handled twice or three times as much business? Ten times as much business? How many more people would you need ? Is your facility large enough, or will you need "growth capital"?

Discuss this in some detail with your partners. Formulate a long-range hiring plan as part of a 'master plan'. Always try to envision beyond your immediate needs.

Writing job descriptions. These are the basic elements of a job description:

- Title of the job (operator, foreman, mechanic, etc.)
- The range of tasks involved in this title
- Educational requirements
- Prior work experience required or desired
- Professional certifications required
- Technical skills required
- Salary range or wage range for this position (should be competitive with similar jobs in your area), and the benefits you offer
- Describes what an exciting place to work this is, and what the opportunities are if a person works here.

As you interview candidates for each position, you should be enthusiastic and positive about the possibilities for advancement. Be prepared to talk about the core values of your company. Show your own passion for your company and see if that passion is shared by the candidate. Make the job description clear and easy to understand.

You must decide whether or not you can tolerate a high turnover rate. A person must be trained and at first, they may not accomplish much. Then if you lose them because they got tired of the job you gave them, or because they found a higher paying job, then you have lost all the time and money you put into training them. In a fast food restaurant, for example, the pay is quite low, there are no gratuities, and employees come in and go out all the time. Training new people to serve customers is a major part of a supervisor's job. Do you want that in your business? How will you prevent what you do not want?

Finding workers.

Workers can come from three sources:

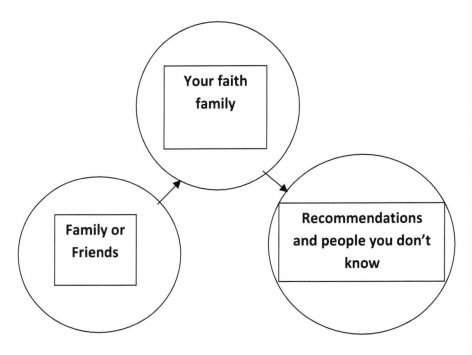

First, look into family members whom you can trust and that you know quite well. The advantages of employing a family member are familiarity and accountability. The disadvantages are the tendency to expect extra favors because they are family members and some difficulty in accepting you as the boss. Another problem is one of seeming fair to all employees, family and non-family. Equal opportunity is important and all employees need to sense that they have a chance for promotion whether they are family members or not. Be careful that the clarity of what is expected is the same whether you are talking to a family member or a good friend, or to someone else. You will have the tendency to be more vague with a family member about what is expected, and much more specific with a non-family member.

Second, look into members of your Christian (or faith) family as possible members of your workforce. The advantages there are some familiarity and hopefully Christian work ethics (honesty, faithfulness, etc.). Other faiths can exhibit the same work ethics too, of course. The disadvantages are often a feeling that they can bend the rules and still be paid (time off to go to religious functions, etc.) and expectation of special favors not given to everyone.

Third, look for people that others recommend or that you meet through advertising for the job through the Internet, walk-ins, word of mouth, newspapers, etc. One day, I put an advertisement in the local newspaper to hire a plant engineer, preferably a mechanical engineer, but open to any with similar training. A young man walked in, and began to talk. Soon, it became obvious that he didn't really want to be an engineer (solve problems, etc) but instead he wanted to drive heavy machinery. We shook hands and he left. A year later he returned, and said he still wanted the engineer job. Another one I had hired in the meantime hadn't worked out. So to fill the need, I hired him for a six-month trial period. The immediate problem was changing out a variety of pumps to replace some that were poorly chosen in the first place. This new engineer did a stellar job, by rapidly becoming a "pump expert", the undisputed "go-to man" in the plant for anything to do with process pumps. I gave him other problems to solve, with other types of equipment, and he did the same thing. He became the "resident expert" in whatever he was assigned. He worked himself into a position of being **indispensable!** He became a permanent employee. He was well compensated for his work. You want people like that working for you! A person who "knows where all the pipes are buried". He was told that "he walked on water" when given his annual performance review.

One risk you have in developing such a person is losing them to a competitor who will offer them twice what you are paying, and then they are suddenly gone. Company loyalty only goes so far. What would you do if this happened in your business?

In all cases, remember that hiring a younger person brings less experience but probably more energy because they may wish to build a future with you. You may have to pay them a little more than the average or they will look for better pay somewhere else so they can support a family. Hiring an older person brings more experience. The danger with either young or old is the tendency of some people to "know more than you do" about your job. This attitude can poison the rest of the group and lead to dissension in your workforce. Be aware of it.

Interviewing and selecting workers.

The interviewing process should be the same whether the applicant is a family member, close friend, a Christian brother or sister, or someone you don't know. Every person should apply for the job in the same way. If it is a person you don't know, then you should telephone them first, with a list of questions. If the candidate seems promising, call them in for a face to face discussion. Here are some typical questions (by no means an exhaustive list):

- Have you read and understood the job description? Any questions about it?
- Why are you interested in this job now?
- Tell me what your experience is which makes you believe that you can do this job well?
- Tell me about any habits you have which could affect your work.
- Tell me about your experience in working both 'for' and 'with' other people.
- What do you consider 'fair treatment' of any employee?
- Why should I hire you and not someone else?

- How flexible are your working hours?
- What sort of pay are you expecting? Benefits expected?
- When can you begin work?
- Is this a temporary job for you or do you prefer to stay a long time?
- What questions do you have about us?

The last question is very important. If the applicant says "no, no questions", then I wonder about his/her intelligence or actual interest In my company. I wonder If perhaps they have other offers they are more interested in and aren't telling me about. I see curiosity as a very important trait, and lack of it as a warning sign.

There are many other questions of course, but this is a start. Be equally honest and frank with every person. When companies hire an employee, they look for someone who satisfies three of the company needs. It can be illustrated like this

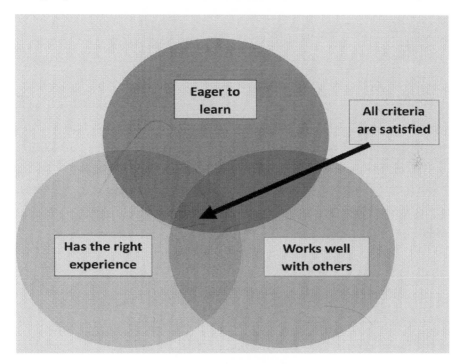

If the candidate meets all three requirements, he or she is likely to get the job. You must be certain what is important and what is not so

important. The contents of those three circles varies with your individual needs. Your needs may be quite different.

Consider hiring people under a contract for a brief period of time, terminating in 6-12 months. In this time, you can evaluate the person's performance, and if it is good, then make it permanent, if it is questionable then renew the contract for another 6 months, and if it is not good, then let the contract expire and get someone else

A variation of the contract hire is to have a person (s) on retainer. This allows you to select very valuable people and pay them for 1) availability, 2) responsiveness and 3) their expertise, without having them on the payroll. Such was the experience of Henry Ford, who knew the right person to call when his Model T plant in Dearborn, Michigan lost the main electric generator and the assembly line stopped. He called Charles Steinmetz, GE's Wizard of Schenectady. "Get here immediately!!" Ford screamed!

Steinmetz arrived, surveyed the generator, and asked for a piece of chalk. Climbing a ladder, he made a chalk mark on the huge generator and told the workers to remove that particular cover plate and replace 16 windings from a field coil. They did, and the generator purred like a kitten, and the Model T factory was back in business again. Ford was delighted and told Steinmetz to send him an invoice. Ford's delight stopped when he got the bill for $10,000. Then he was furious and asked Steinmetz to send him another bill, fully itemized to explain why it was so high. That bill explained in two lines:

- Making a chalk mark on the generator. $1
- Knowing where to make the chalk mark. $9,999
- Total $10,000

Ford understood perfectly, and paid the bill gladly. It is essential to your success that you know people of incredible value and who can be called upon when needed. Pay them well.

In one plant that I set up, there were three machines which were the centerpieces of the operation. Two months after start up, the first one broke. The next month, the second one broke. Then the third one broke. While there had been an agreement with the equipment supplier that they were responsible for the machines we bought from them, they disavowed any responsibility for these three catastrophic events. Surely, we must have done something wrong! I had a "Steinmetz" at my disposal, who examined the situation. He made a list of 12 possible reasons why this could have happened. Together, we took the list to the equipment manufacturer and presented it to them. Could it have been reason number 1? No. Reason number 2? No. He reduced the list to only one possible cause: you didn't machine it properly, and therefore under our agreement, you owe us a quick replacement for all three lines. They had to comply. Those lines have now been running for more than 30 years. I had a "Steinmetz" of very high value at my disposal. Do you?

The principles above could apply to anything from a sewing machine, a car, a coffee maker, a computer or anything else your business depends on.

Managing compensation (wages and salaries).

There are many different ways to administer the pay scales of all of your workers (numbers are for example only):

One common way is to construct pay ranges:
- Level 1 responsibility or skill level pays 1000 to 2000
- Level 2 responsibility or skill level pays 2000 to 3000
- Level 3 responsibility or skill level pays 3000 to 4000

This way, a new employee starts at the bottom of the pay scale, and proves they can do the job well and gets pay raises. They can look ahead and see that upon exemplary performance, they can move over into the next level. It also gives you, the owner of the business, some latitude about paying employees based on their performance, and allows you to compare to what others in the same industry are paying so that you can stay competitive for the best workers.

If workers and/or salaried people are asked to work overtime, or on holidays or weekends, then you must consider how you will pay them extra. If the standard work week is 40 hours, set by the government department of labor, and the employee works 50 hours, how much will they be paid? In some European countries, the work week is 35 hours with almost 2 months paid vacation each year. How would you staff for that?

In addition to the monthly or weekly wages and salaries, you should consider a bonus system. If a worker does a wonderful job at something which truly helps the company, and was not part of their job description, then you have a reserve from which you can publicly honor that employee with a special bonus. This gives incentive to the other employees to try to excel at what they do, and think more broadly about benefiting the company as a whole.

Managing worker benefits

- You will need a system in which each employee receives a benefit package which the company can afford and is an incentive to work for you. These benefits vary and often include:
- Vacation time (paid or unpaid)
- Health care
- A system for putting aside savings in a safe place (A Thrift Plan, for example)
- A retirement package
- Health facilities in the workplace
- Safe places to park motorbikes and cars
- Family counseling
- Partnership in the company (becoming part-owners)

These items should be in writing and explained well to an incoming employee to avoid any misunderstanding. In many cultures, funerals of even remote family members are very important and can involve many days off from work. Have an understanding in writing with each employee how you would handle this. Are those time offs paid or not paid? How will you replace that individual when he or she leaves for such a purpose?

Treating workers fairly and retaining them

Every workplace has issues between workers and those in management. You will need to set up a clear system of handling worker grievances. Such issues as:

- Failure to pay for overtime hours
- Arguments between workers
- Working conditions
- Bad health environment
- Dispute between workers and the bosses
- Favoritism between workers and bosses

How to handle those who prove incompetent to do a job versus those who show great skill and whose output is far superior

- How to handle sick days
- A person whose child is sick and they have to call and not come in to work.

These and many others are commonplace and you as the owner need to think about how you would handle them if they arise.

Advice for employee issues.

Handle each issue promptly. Do not let it develop into a larger issue

Have someone in your business who is especially good at it, handle the issues. If you are not good at it, don't insist on doing it when there is someone more astute available to act as arbitrator.

Never demean or embarrass an employee for bringing a complaint to you.

Make each employee feel valuable and productive as much as possible

You must not put up with dissention in the workforce. If someone is talking badly about the way the business is run, talk to that person right away.

If company core values are being violated, correct them right away. These may be grounds for dismissal. Such things as:

- Horseplay, fighting, other physical altercations
- Blatant safety violation
- Theft of company goods
- Tampering with the company's financial books and records
- Sexual harassment
- Giving away company property or company secrets or ideas
- Unauthorized use of company equipment for personal use
- Poor use of company time for personal reasons (cell phone, texting, etc.)
- Alcohol and drugs on the job
- Insubordination

Chapter 2 records the experience of Emma, the granddaughter who successfully sold more Girl Scout cookies than all the others in her troupe combined, by applying her creativity. However, the final chapter of that story was left untold. It belongs here in the subject of "fairness". While Emma did an extraordinary job, her girl scout leader thought that it was not "fair" for Emma to be so richly rewarded while others were not, as it might 'offend' some of the other girls who were lazy and sold nothing! So while Emma was thanked for her hard and clever work, the leader added up all the cookies sold by the entire group, Emma's 2000 plus a total of 150 by all the others, divided the total by the number of girls(10), got the average and declared that <u>every</u> girl had sold 215 boxes of cookies and stated that no one person would get an award, but the whole team would be rewarded; the lazy ones as well as the others!! How inspired do you think Emma would be each year unless her creativity is recognized as special and appropriately rewarded? What incentive is there for the other girls to do better next year, if Emma is going to do most of the work anyway?

Your employees will respond the same way if you recognize their contributions and ideas. Otherwise, you create a socialist system which has yet to be shown to work well anywhere in the world! This practice of "fairness" is absolutely TOXIC!

Toxic "fairness"

Takes me places in my heart that I don't want to go:

Bitterness

Anger

Bad decisions based on emotions

Bad priorities become the top priorities

Brings out my basic, sinful nature

How do you deal with a sinful nature?
(I John 1:9)

Why is it always better to have contented employees? *Vineyard parable*

Being fair does not always mean being equal. Always reward those who have made significant contributions and recognize them in a public way! That will incentivise others to improve.

How can you manage your workforce when business drops or is erratic and unpredictable?

There are times when the orders do not come in as you had planned. You have the staff ready, but the work level is quite a bit lower than expected. You as owner of the business need to make it one of your priorities to stay informed about your business in general and to know what the trends are. A successful business person can anticipate problems ahead and be ready for them. Joseph showed this management skill in dealing with the famine of Egypt which was about to overtake the country (Genesis 41). What do you do with employees whose normal jobs have gone away for a while due to lack of business?

The most common way to deal with this problem is in these steps:

Find other useful jobs for employees to do if there are no orders to fill. They can clean, paint, repair, etc. This is a solution if the drop In business is of short duration.

If necessary, then lay off employees temporarily in order of lowest seniority, with the least time employee being the first to go. Save that job for them once business picks back up.

Firing employees

The steps to firing an employee are begun in section G-F above. You will need clear and ample proof, even witnesses, to build a case to fire a person. Only when you have hard evidence should you approach the person and confront him or her with it. Once it is concluded that the person has broken key rules in the company, then fire them right away, and escort them out of the property. Other reasons for firing someone than those above in G-F, are

162

disruptiveness, and failure to produce results. The more you have kept in writing, the better. This will save you from a contest of one word against another.

Words of wisdom

The idea of rotating jobs so that everyone has a little practice in doing every job, is generally not a good idea. Not everyone enjoys or is skilled at every job. It is better to keep someone in an assignment in which they are happy and productive.

There are times in business when you feel very alone and frustrated. In those times, you need a partner who knows enough about your business to come in and ask you the really tough questions. Have you got such a partner?

When you hire people, remember the importance of chemistry. Someone who works for you, must not work 'against' you. Hire people who you feel you can get along with, and who are as committed to the business as you are. During the interview process, it's fine to look at the interviewee and say "so, tell me a good joke".

When interviewing, ask where the interviewee fits into the family. Try to ascertain if this person grew up learning how to share and get along with others.

A good interview needs to include enough questions to see if they will take any initiative, or whether they work entirely on being told what to do. What kind of person do you want?

If there are any local organizations, such as Young Entrepreneurs, it is advisable to join it. Meeting other people is very valuable if they are faced with problems similar to yours. These organizations should also get you contacts with the local government officials. You need to know how to work with them well. The old adage that "it isn't what you know that helps you, but who you know," is true.

In putting together your workforce, beware of people who "know more than you do". They tend to be unteachable, and will likely cause problems. You do want to build confidence, but it is YOUR business and you don't want someone who undermines what you decide or say to the rest of the workforce.

Looking at the company life cycle, on page 100. You must understand that in stage 1, in which you are the only employee, you have managed nothing as yet. It is in stage 2 that you learn how to manage! In stage 3, you are identifying and training others to manage for you, while you manage the managers.

Be flexible enough to accommodate a person who starts in one area of your business, but upon seeing another area, might want to try it out and find even more contentment with their job.

In some cases, weekly wage employees have been paid on Friday at noon so they can go to the bank during the lunch hour; then they don't come back until Monday morning!

Interviewing is not a popularity contest, but an effort to see how well a person can meet your needs. Are they qualified, or not?

Do not over promise about job security. Most employment is done on the basis that the employee can quit the job with a short notice, and the company can fire them with a short notice.

Always put your senior (in experience, not age) people in charge of training others who will work for them. A foreman should train his/her operators, for example.

Worker productivity is an important part of hiring and keeping the right people for the job, so you can hire the minimum number of workers. This will keep you competitive on cost margin against your competitors. The place to start is to hire people who show enthusiasm for the job, good understanding of the assignments, and ability to work well with others. Find ways to measure your productivity. It could be number of clients/day, number of kg/hour, number of orders per hour, or other ways to track productivity in your business.

Who has the final decision? This may be obvious in some cultures, but not in others. For example, in Ivory Coast, it is commonly believed that the oldest person in the village, or in the company, has the final say simply because of 'gray hair'. But if the company is yours, and it has been entrusted by God to you for stewardship, then you should make the final decisions. When you hire people to work for you then, it is important to have clear understanding about who has the final word on important decisions. It might be good to explain a RACI chart to your employees about how you plan to operate this business:

1. **R** = responsibility. Who has the responsibility for each task and each decision? Responsible to get the work done on time.
2. **A** = accountability. Who will be held accountable for something getting done? Has the ultimate ownership of the task at hand.
3. **C** = consultation. With whom must I consult before doing the task?
4. **I** = inform. Whom must I inform before going ahead with a task?

	Person 1	Person 2	Person 3
R	Responsibility to do task		
A		If the job doesn't get done, it is his/her fault!	
C			Check with me first just to make sure.
I	I am ready to do task, and then when it is done.		

The RACI chart gives you, as owner of the business, the basis for discipline. This is especially useful when the cultural norm is for the older person to always be 'right' in their judgments.

The RACI chart, clearly communicated, answers such questions about hiring an older brother, who needs a job, for example. Some cultures demand that if an older brother needs a job, and you have a business, that you give him a job!

At what point in your business should you have a board of directors over you, to keep you accountable and to provide you with advice. These could be considered people in the "C" category, people with whom you consult on a regular basis.

In some cultures, kickbacks are common as a way to do business. For example, perhaps the chief of the village must give his permission for you to build your small place of business, and has the authority to say 'yes' or 'no 'over which land you will use. In order to gain his permission, his "fee" for using his authority may be that you hire all of his out-of-work family members. These family workers are neither needed nor qualified, but you must hire them anyway. How will you respond?

I ordered very expensive, high quality equipment to be shipped from Germany to another country in which I was building a plant. Upon entering the port, I was told that I must wait at least a week for all that equipment to be taken off the ship, inspected, papers filed, etc. "It's a very big ship, you know!" Baffled, and unused to such stalling, I decided to pay a "tip" to speed up the process. The equipment was off the ship and onto a waiting flatbed truck that very afternoon! The "tip" consisted of several cartons of Marlboros.

When that same flatbed arrived at the final destination, about 500 miles from the port, it was parked. Immediately and out of nowhere, about 30 people with almost no clothes, each hoping to be paid a dollar, showed up trying to shove the equipment off the end of the truck and onto the ground! Horrified at the potential loss and damage, I was able to stop that "help" from happening and get more professional help to unload properly. How would you have handled that? Suppose I had not been there?

I encourage a system by which each employee at any level be given a one-on-one, face to face performance review. This should be done whether it is your business and you have one employee, or a

166

hundred. This is meant to be a constructive discussion (not a destructive one). This discussion should be interactive, exchanging ideas of the past 6 months or 12-month performance on the job, and then a discussion of how the employee can improve. All parts of the discussion must be carefully noted in writing and signed by both. Some call this a "performance review", and others call it "a discussion of contribution". I prefer the latter. With each work assignment, there should be metrics by which the employee's accomplishments can be measured. The discussion of performance looks at these assignments and grades them, and determines the level of responsibility that this person is capable of. Part of the meeting needs to be devoted to the future plans for this employee. It is very important that the employee feels that he/she has a future and is a contributing member of the staff.

People tell you things about themselves, to make themselves look 'marvelous'. Some people are very good at this, and are able to make you agree to something (like hiring them) before you have had a chance to "fact-check" to make sure what they say is true. A good friend of mine was editor for the Associated Press, and told me this 'factual story'. It seems that a large truck was loaded with chickens and had an accident on one of the major highways. The story was covered by a young, aspiring news reporter who couldn't wait to have his first exciting story! The truck overturned on the highway, he reported, and the traffic had to stop and witness the scene of thousands of chickens running all over the highway, feathers everywhere!! What a mess!! The reporter was so excited. But when the facts all came to light, it was a slightly different story. A truck full of chickens DID overturn, traffic was indeed interrupted, but the chickens were…frozen chickens! Feathers? No, not quite. Running all over the highway? Not exactly! The young reporter's career was tainted forevermore. Be careful that you don't hire people to work for you who tell you "what happened in the shop or factory" without getting their facts correct and checked! You do not want to take action based on incorrect information!

Finally, the criteria for getting the right people for the job are these three "C"s:

- Character: Does this person demonstrate a godly character, one whom you can trust, who tells the truth, who is willing to assume personal responsibility even if they are admitting to a mistake and who will be a strong testimony of behavior to other employees and customers?
- Competence: Is this person able to demonstrate that he/she knows what they are doing? Do they learn quickly? Do they think before they act?
- Compatibility: Can this person work well with others? Does he/she show that they are a healer and not a divider? Are they a team player?

Job Description Template

A certain business needs warehouse workers. Make a sketch of the operation as you envision it, mark on the sketch where people would work, then write a job description for that job which you will use to interview and hire people. Sample job description:

- Description: Warehouse Worker
- Warehouse Worker Job Purpose: Completes shipments by processing and loading orders.
- Warehouse Worker Job Duties:
- Prepares orders by processing requests and supply orders; pulling materials; packing boxes; place orders in delivery area.
- Completes delivery by driving truck or van to & from vendors.
- Maintains truck or van by completing preventive maintenance requirements; arranging for repairs.
- Maintains inventory controls by collecting stock location orders and printing requests.
- Maintains quality service by following organization standards.
- Maintains safe and clean work environment by keeping shelves, pallet area, and workstations neat; maintaining a clean shipping supply area; complying with procedures, rules, and regulations.
- Completes reports by entering required information.
- Maintains technical knowledge by attending educational workshops; reviewing publications.
- Contributes to team effort by accomplishing related results as needed.

Skills/Qualifications: Teamwork, Coordination, Organization, Planning, Time Management, Reporting Skills, Inventory Control, Documentation Skills, Equipment Maintenance, Data Entry Skills, Dependability

---

Exercises

1. Create Your Own Set Of Job Descriptions Based On The Business You Have Described In Your Business Plan !

- Finances
- Sales & marketing
- Managing
- Operations
- Handling people
- Handling customers
- Engineering, R&D
- Purchasing
- Advertising
- Security

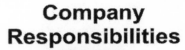

Company Responsibilities

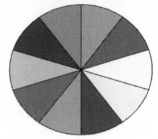

2. Using This Pie Chart, Describe The Types Of Functions Which May Take Place In Your Business, And Decide Which Ones You Will Do, And Which Ones You Think It Better To Hire Another Person To Do.   Are You Really Good At All Of These? No. Do You Really Have Time For All Of These? No.

Go back to the discussion about managers, technicians and entrepreneurs. You must honestly decide which one you are. If you want your business to grow and do not feel that you have the attributes of an entrepreneur, then think about hiring one on retainer.

Powerful Questions

The success and sustainability of your business is largely dependent on the people who work with you and for you. One "bad apple" in the basket can spoil the whole basket if left unattended to or unrecognized. Therefore we need practice and knowhow in how to properly address peoples' needs, complaints, issues, etc. In his wonderful book "Leadership Coaching" , by Tony Stoltzfus, he discusses how to ask "Powerful Questions". You as the entrepreneur or manager should not hesitate to interview each employee informally as often as needed, and engage with them one-on-one to discern what the troubles may be. KNOW your employees well! I

170

have seen businesses fall apart because the boss who once knew them and their families, ceased doing that and acted as if he no longer cared, and the employees' felt disconnected. That is the beginning of trouble. In most countries, especially in Latin America and East Asia, personal relationships are extremely important.

When engaging with an employee, don't waste time asking questions which are open ended, or can be answered by a simple, dodgy, "yes" or "no" or "OK". The common question "how are you?" usually does not want an answer. When a person opens up and talks with you, take the time to do that well and ask questions that require some thought. It also requires you to be a good listener! Examples:

Jesus asked his disciples "Who do you say that I am? Matthew 16:15. Good question!! Can't be answered with a yes, no or maybe. Another question from Jesus was "What can I do for you?" referring to the woman at the well. His questions were always directed at the other person, showing interest in them. Think about asking these questions:

What are some of the barriers that prevent you from moving ahead?

- What can I do for you?
- What do you need to do in the next week to meet your goal?
- How do you know this?
- What are your main concerns?
- Am I missing something in what you've told me?
- What do you think is the best way to resolve this challenge?
- How can we find some things upon which we agree, rather than those which divide us?

There are many others. The key is to listen well and exhibit genuine curiosity. Another book which covers this topic well is "Fierce Conversations" by Susan Scott.

Improper Questions

Questions can be asked in the wrong way too. These will not set the stage for getting the proper answer or the truthful answer and will lead your interview off the track or the intended purpose quickly. Think about you would respond to such questions. These questions apply to both an interview for a job, as well as talking to one of your employees about resolving an issue with the business.

- Avoid leading questions: So why are you so overweight? Perhaps you need better, more healthy habits or more exercise?
- Avoid closed questions: How are you doing today? Simple answer is "fine". With such a question, you are getting nowhere.
- Avoid judgmental questions: You haven't been doing a very good job lately, have you? Puts people in the defense right away.
- Avoid advice questions: have you thought about a better maintenance program, or hiring a new mechanic? It gives advice instead of making the person think about what they could do to solve the problem.
- Avoid "why" questions: Why didn't you think of this sooner? Again, puts the person on the defensive and they have to protect themselves instead of coming up with some useful solutions.
- Avoid small questions: How did you sleep last night? This question has little or nothing to do with an issue you may want more information for.
- Avoid guilt questions: I've told you several times to watch what you're doing, and you did It anyway! Again this throws the person Into a defensive position and the truth won't come out.

Chapter 7 Executive Summary

Subject:	Your Executive Summary
Lesson Objectives:	1. Understand what an executive summary is and how it helps in selling the concept of your business to potential investors. 2. Students will develop their own executive summary, and defend it to the instructors
Books Recommended	"The Everything Business Plan Book", Windhaus and Ramsey

Introduction

You have completed your modules on creativity, feasibility, developed a business plan with all of its components, and a human resources plan. It is now time to summarize all of your work so that you can present your proposal to a lending institution and potential partners.

Following is a good example of an executive summary, using chicha morada drink as the model. The name of the company is Inca Chicha, Ltd. An outline of what you are about to write is:

- Subject matter.... What is this report about?
- Methods of analysis... What work did you do to arrive at these conclusions?
- Findings... What did you find as you did this study?
- Conclusions... Based on the above findings, what can you conclude? Include your financial conclusion.
- Recommendations.... Based on this conclusion, what do you recommend?
- Limitations of this report.... Explain what further work may have to be done, if any.
- Request.... What are you asking for?

Executive Summaries (Examples)

Inca Chicha, Ltd

This report provides an analysis and a recommendation for the formation of a new company, Inca Chicha, Ltd. This will include the financing needed, the profitability expected and any risks that might be incurred. The product will be purple corn drink, sold by the bottle both retail and wholesale.

The analysis methods used marketing surveys, decision and risk analyses, cost of operations calculations and extensive research of the business climate and competitive conditions in the area. The time horizon is 5 years as a basis for our conclusions. All calculations can be found in the appendix.

This study concludes that the prospects of earning a profit with the sales of chicha morada are good, and that after modest investment and start up, the business will be positive cash flow in 2 years. Investors can expect to get returns on their money during the second year, get their principle fully returned in five years, and earn profits thereafter at the rate of about 8% per year. It is intended that the company will take all profits after distributions and reinvest in new corn fields, thereby expanding their business volume. Our vision is that the business will grow at 15% per year in volumes and sales revenues. Our primary advertising tool will be our website.

The recommendation is that capital be used to build a small building 4kms from Huanuco, Peru, which will include the production area and the offices and sales areas. This will give us room for expansion in the future, and is a heavily used area which is known to most people in town. We believe that the company name, Inca Chicha, Ltd, is also recognizable and attractive.

From this point forward, we propose to monitor competition and to solidify our chances of buying future land upon which to grow more corn. We also propose to sell only one product at this time. Other products may get further consideration, but not now.

We are hereby requesting a loan of $500,000 to buy the necessary land, build the building and the process equipment for purifying and bottling our product. We expect to provide 24 new jobs in the area.

Edward S. Rowse and the Inca Chicha team, 15 May, 2013

What is absent from this summary? It fails to mention anything about spiritual impact on the community. It also leaves out any continuing need for money to support the business in the early times when it is not earning a profit. The number one thing which is not clearly stated is payback. When will those who loaned money, be fully repaid? It would also be helpful to mention how many years' experience the business has by simply working on the street. The investor will ask "how much of this drink have you sold so far?" Finally, it would be good to mention what kind of profit margin is seen for this product, stating what it may cost to produce one hundred bottles compared to how much revenue for the same.

This executive summary is not a very good example because it leaves too many unanswered questions.

The Bridge School

We propose to start a school called "The Bridge School", to be located in downtown Sao Paulo, Brazil. It will provide continuing education for persons recently graduated from a university. Herein you will find the financing needed, the profitability expected and any risks that might be incurred.

We are asking for a capital loan of 450,000 reais, and plan to supply an additional 250,000 reais from our own resources. This will be needed in 3 months' time from now. In addition, we will need a loan of 50,000 reais six months from now, for startup expenses and some initial working capital. We will also need to establish a credit line of 30,000 reais per year for 4 years, starting 12 months from now, until the operation of the school becomes stable. We expect to pay back all of these loans 5 years after start up in September, 2020.

Our school will be established in rented offices. By the third year of operation, we expect to have 275 students per year enrolled for the one-year program. These students will pay 80,000 reais each. After 8 years of experience, we plan to set up a second school in the Sao Paulo area.

The school will be operated with a staff of ten, full time people. There will be one director, one manager, one financial officer, one recruiter and six marketing staff. We also plan to advertise using local newspapers. The faculty will be all part time. Some will be foreigners who teach English. Others will be nationals who teach the other curriculum outlined in the feasibility report. All will be paid salary.

Once the school begins, we must protect it from failure. Our strategy is to monitor the needs of the students and change as those needs change, so that we do not fall below the minimum 200 enrollment. We also will cooperate with local universities in a way that does not duplicate what they are doing, but rather is complimentary to them, so that they will send graduates in our direction. Should this plan fail, we will have little assets to dispose of and will pay off any remaining loans.

This plan will enrich our community, help our graduates find good jobs in the workplace, and strengthen our nation. The full business plan is available to you.

Respectfully submitted: The Bridge School team, April 1, 2019

How could this executive summary be improved to include essentials which are left out? What are some questions that the readers will surely have?

1. First, there is no mention of any name who will be the person in charge or the person responsible to see that this program succeeds.
2. Second, the capital request is rather large. What do they plan to use that money for?
3. Third, this sounds like a plan that must have been tried many times before. How certain are they that there are not many other schools like this in the area, and if this school were to be established, how could those competitors prevent you from growing or even getting started?
4. Fourth, is there any plan to merge with another school in the area in the future?
5. Fifth, there is no mention of a spiritual impact plan.
6. Sixth, what further work needs to be done before we can secure a loan?

Custom Shirts

I am a self-employed entrepreneur and have been making customized shirts for people in my local community of Korhogo, Cote d'Ivoire for six years. My business has been growing slowly but surely, and with my daughter's help, we can make and sell 10 shirts per month, operating out of my home. There is an opportunity to sell twice that many if I could make other styles of shirts. To do that, I need to invest $500 to buy a second sewing machine. Now, when I get a request for such a design, I must refer them to a man across town who has the right type of machine. I have studied the market carefully and am convinced that I can make up to 20 shirts per month, and sell them at a higher price, if I was properly equipped. My daughter is my partner, and she has the technical skills to operate this machine, and we can still do this in our home. This past year, I sold 132 shirts at a revenue of $1320, and a profit margin of $126. If I had a second machine, I could realize the sales of 211 shirts per year, at a revenue of $2505, and a profit margin of $591, thus increasing our profit margin by more than 4 times! By doing this, I have enriched the quality and value of my merchandise significantly. My daughter and I also serve the Lord and will honor Him with our business and be known even more than now as Christians who treat people well and give them what they need in a timely fashion. I also realize that the new type of shirts require different materials, and I have established that my supply chain for both the new style and the old style is intact by opening up a second source for all of the various components.

We will pay back the loan in 3 years. I may need to come back in a year to borrow another $500 to improve the safety and security of our place of business, but for now, we are secure against disruption. I also may come back and borrow another $500 for a third sewing machine, but that will depend on how our business grows.

Thank you for your consideration, and the full business plan is available upon request.

This is a powerful example of a "no-brainer". This lady should easily get her loan, and even try hard to pay it ahead of schedule. She leaves no doubt who is in charge, she gives you confidence that between she and her daughter she has the technical expertise, she assures that the market demand is there and that the prices are right, and she simply needs the right equipment to do her job well. There is some allusion to others doing the same thing and nothing about how they will compete with her. There is also a statement that she has considered her supply chain and secured it. She has a track record of six successful years in the business already.

This is a great presentation and if I were a bank, I'd loan her the money! I might even ask her if she'd like to have an invested partner, and GIVE her the money in return for 20% equity in the business. She is even in a position to cut her prices a little, in case competition becomes tight.

Finally, it is good to notice that this enterprise is in a small town. The mayor of the town told me that when a young person is able to move away, they do it as soon as possible, because "there is nothing here in this town for me". They all go south to Abidjan, a very large city, where they think they can "strike it rich". What a joy to know that this lady is a good example of how such a town can hold out the hope of a job! Perhaps others can open up other businesses in that town. Her pastor prays for her too!

Investor Questions

This lady (and you) must be prepared to answer several questions which will be asked of her during an interview with a bank, or a private investor. Such questions as these are almost guaranteed to be asked:

1. Please give me a clear statement of your purpose and your goals
2. What experience do you and your team (coworkers) have in this job?
3. Where are your competitive advantages?
4. Tell me why this is a good idea financially.
5. Describe a clear path between your startup and sustainability.
6. How much of your own money are you willing to invest in this idea? Having some of your own money in the proposal Is always reassuring to an investor.
7. Who are the other investors who will keep your business stable?
8. What are the risks which could give you trouble if they happened?
9. How flexible is your business model? How can you grow if the demand is high?
10. How do you plan to distribute your retained earnings?
11. Describe how you will manage your accounts receivable and account payable?
12. When can we expect to get our money back?
13. Has this idea already worked in other places?
14. Is there another technology which could displace you?
15. Rather than loan you the money, are you will willing to accept the money and give me a certain share equity in your business, as your partner?
16. How many such products (or services) have you sold already and what margin or mark-up do you have on them?

Chapter 8 Why do so many businesses fail?

Subject:	Why so many businesses fail
Lesson Objectives:	To review why 75% of business startups fail, and what can we learn from those experiences in order to prevent us from repeating the same thing.
Books Recommended	"Success God's Way", Dr. Charles Stanley "The Emyth Revisited, why most small businesses don't work and what to do about it", Michael Gerber

Introduction

There are numerous reasons why businesses fail. Some fail sooner than others. We all acknowledge that we should learn from the mistakes of the past, but we seldom take those to heart and learn from them. Instead, we too often repeat them. The aim of this chapter is to put the spotlight on why nearly 75% of all startups and even longer standing businesses fail. Shall we all agree that we do NOT want to start a business that has a high likelihood of failing? Why waste time, money and energy on a loser? This chapter is the product of much research into this topic and I share it with you, the reader, for your benefit. Part of this research has been gained by the author, listening to the ideas of people from around the world and seeking guidance and help. Please read these ideas carefully and predict what will happen.

Adding Value?

A man from Nigeria was touring the United States, and witnessed the use of water filters. He became quite familiar with the way they work, removing harmful particulates and trace contaminants from the drinking water. The result was better tasting and healthier water.

The idea occurred to him about the needs in his home country, especially in the rural villages. He gathered several models and designs of water filters and took them home. He approached many households and thought for sure that mothers especially would see the health value for their family. When he demonstrated the filters, the mothers would say "these are supposed to improve the health of my children? Look around you. Do my children look sick? No, they are playing like normal children. Take your gadgets and go!" The mothers could not see the value of the filters. His business idea crashed. Fortunately, he didn't actually go into a business selling filters without first trying the market. Some people would have signed on as a manufacturer's representative, bought a large inventory, hoping then to sell it and recoup their money and make a profit.

I have witnessed many places in the world in which fruit is sold on tables, attended by a lady (usually), who hopes that someone will step up and buy from them. Mangoes are often sold that way, for example. One lady has a table set up with a pile of mangoes. Next to her is another lady, also selling mangoes. Next to her is yet another lady selling mangoes. Why, then, would another person set up a fourth table, and showing no differences from the others, try to sell mangoes also? What value would they add by doing that?

There is a fruit stand in an upscale district (Belgrano) of Buenos Aires, Argentina. All of the fruit is cleaned and neatly stacked in pyramids, and is rather expensive.

Not far away is another fruit stand, in which the fruit is not cleaned, and is piled randomly. The fruit is considerably less costly than the first fruit stand. People walking by both stands, especially mothers pushing baby carriages or with small children, almost always buy from the more expensive dealer. They gladly, unhesitatingly pay more for the clean, neatly piled fruit. The perception is that their families deserve the best and price should not stand in the way. But all the fruit come from the same sources, same trees !!

Value is a perception. The more organized, cleaner fruit, while the same as the other, is perceived to have higher value! Why not pay half as much, and wash it?

The Charcoal Pit restaurant (mentioned earlier) in my area of Delaware has two stores. One is nostalgic in being the same décor as it was at startup in 1956. It plays old music of the era; its hamburgers are high quality and the prices always reasonable. Most of all, it is quiet and relaxing.

The other restaurant across town and of the same name is a noisy sports bar with distracting televisions all over the walls.

The atmosphere is far less appealing to me. I will pay more to go to the first one than the second. The value is in the ambiance. Happy customers are like perennial flowers; they keep coming back!

A good cup of coffee is available down the street for $0.89. But I would prefer to drive three times as far to get a Starbuck's coffee for $4.00! Why? It doesn't really taste better. I like it because it identifies me as a Starbuck's patron. It just sounds better. In my perception, it has higher value. In reality, it doesn't.

My aunt was a famous portrait artist in Santa Fe, New Mexico. Her portraits usually were by commission, sold to people who wanted a loved one to sit for her and have a portrait done. Occasionally, she would see an interesting "head", and paint that person and hang it for sale in a gallery.

One hung there with a $1500 price tag for several months. No one wanted to buy it. The owner of the gallery suggested that my aunt make a change. She thought he meant to lower the price; yes, of course, slash the price to $750. Instead, he added another zero, pricing it at $15,000. The painting sold the next day!! You see, no one wants a silly $1500 portrait to hang in their home for guests to admire; they want a $15,000 portrait to be admired!

One reason businesses fail is they can no longer deliver the "value" that the consumer wants. That value may be in a name, or quality, in feeding your pride, in ambience or service. If your company can convince the buying public that you deliver consistently high value which is important to them, <u>you can expect to minimize the risk of failure.</u>

<u>People buy things for their own reasons, not yours.</u> If you think that people will be your customers because they feel sorry for you, you are wrong. You will fail.

There are many other reasons for business failure. The previous discussion about value can be restated as 'failure to differentiate your product or service". Why would people buy from you instead of someone else?

Market Changes

Another top reason for failure is misunderstanding the needs of the customer, and not changing as the needs of customers change. The lady who made shirts understood the needs well, and met those needs. The needs changed, and her offering changed. She thrived.

Some failures happen because the business finds itself in a mature or saturated market, and you have only a small share. The people selling mangoes on tables side by side find themselves in a situation where everybody is doing the same thing and a newcomer to that same business in that same place can't command much share of the market.

Location

Poor location is another reason for failure. The lady in Nepal who owned the jewelry business was poorly located for retail sales until she changed her marketing strategy. Only locals passed by her store, and they don't buy. Tourists buy, but not in that part of town. When she decided to sell primarily to overseas wholesalers, she began to succeed. Then it didn't much matter where she was located. But she found wholesaling a different world from retailing!

Financial Management

Poor financial management is going to cause failure for a number of reasons.

186

Costs, income and cash flow are poorly documented and usually misunderstood, so those who own the business are Forecasting and Planning blind to what is happening.

Mishandling of the profits in the business leads to not knowing where the money went.

Dishonest use of the company's money will sink the company if not quickly and decisively corrected. Treating the company's money as your own, embezzlement, corruption, etc must be dealt with.

Going into high debt, borrowing too much unnecessarily or prematurely, or agreeing to pay high interest on loans instead of shopping around to secure the best deal, will lead to failure.

Misunderstanding the differences between fixed cost and variable cost will cause you to make bad decisions. If your business is too greatly burdened with fixed cost, then when business is down it will be harmful.

Having no leverage in your supply chain can lead to no options when costs reduce your margins to low or zero. If a supply cost increases, do you have other options, or are you unable to buy from someone else to keep your business supplied?

Deciding to borrow everything you need to start the business should be avoided. Save up enough to put a lot of your own money into the capital needed to start and run the business, and borrow as little as possible. Buying instead of renting space is much preferred. It has been said often that the only person who makes a profit is the landlord!

Put your own energy and hours into the affairs of the business before hiring someone to do work that you can do, especially in the beginning of your business. Keep your initial costs down!

Forecasting and Planning

Poor planning and poor forecasting of volumes, prices, costs, profit margins will also cause the business to fail. Using inaccurate numbers to base budgets on will lead to failure, as will poor decisions about managing inventory and hiring people you really don't need yet. Put off hiring people until you absolutely need them. You want the Lord to bless your business and use it for his glory. Just as you learn to tithe of your business income, you should look forward to giving away money for just causes. Here is an example of one man, Waldemar Schroeder, who resides in Germany. He has become wealthy from a very successful clock business. The Lord impressed upon him the need to help orphans in Eastern Europe, especially in Ukraine. He has a good friend who is an architect and another who is a construction contractor. Together they have formed a NGO business entity "Bridges to Life Foundation". In cooperation with the Ukrainian government, and with the Baptist Churches of Ukraine, Mr. Schroeder designs and builds homes suitable for 12 orphans. As the church donates land close to the church, and as the church arranges for a man and wife to become "parents" of the orphans and dwell in the house with the children, ages 2 to 18, and as the church provides general oversight of the families, then the government chooses which orphans to relocate from decidedly substandard state orphanages and places them in these beautiful facilities. It is a win-win for everyone and the results have been spectacular! More than 50 such houses have been built, and more are to come in all parts of the country. The government pays the couples about $100 per orphan per month to feed, house, clothe and sustain the "family". In this way, a successful, German businessman is showing the love of Christ with his wealth. This is part of God's sustainability plan!

Two, new orphanages in Korosten, Ukraine, built by "Bridges to Life Foundation" on the property of Grace Baptist Church. A set of parents and 12 orphans in each building

Adding Value

Principle: People buy things for their reasons, not yours. Examples:

1. Jewelry in Nepal

2. My aunt's paintings

3. Starbuck's coffee

4. Mango Berry versus Berri Yummi

5. Oranges piled on a table

6. McDonald's French Fries

7. Water filters in Ivory Coast

8. What do you offer that adds value?

Chapter 9 Plan to sustain your business.

Subject:	Planning to Sustain your Business
Lesson Objective:	How to keep your business afloat
Books Recommended	"Out of the Crisis" W. Edwards Deming "The Lean Startup" Eric Ries

Introduction

The story of the Titanic is well known, historically and thanks to the movie. While much of the movie was fictional, the events surrounding this "unsinkable" ship, are well documented.

Titanic 1912

The ship was indeed made at the Belfast shipyards in 1911, by master builders, and commanded by the British fleet, the largest in the world at that time. But in their rush to become rich and famous, the ship was left not quite finished before she was loading the first passengers, and set sail in the month of April, 1912.

To make the matters worse, since the unsinkability of the ship was "guaranteed" (God Himself cannot sink this ship!!), many other shortcuts were made which doomed it. With about 2200 people aboard, it set sail from Southhampton heading for a four-day journey across the North Atlantic. It did so with only half the number of lifeboats needed to carry all of the passengers, to cater to the wishes of the especially wealthy aboard the ship who found them 'unsightly'. After all, look at this beautiful ship! And, to make it even better, our skipper is Captain Edward J. Smith, who has 43 years of experience crossing the ocean in every month of the year. We are in such safe hands! Yes, April is iceberg season, with the monsters falling off the Greenland glaciers and floating silently south. The officers on the bridge that fateful night on April 15 didn't have binoculars because someone forgot to put them aboard. Going at a higher than planned speed, with all engines running full, the iceberg appeared and it was too late to avoid it. Five of the compartments of the double hull were peeled open like a giant can opener. Had only four ripped open, the boat would have stayed afloat and limped into New York. But the weight of five compartments full of sea water doomed the ship. It sank it in about 2 hours, with 1500 people dying. Only 700 were saved. They were totally unprepared!

So many businesses fail because they are unprepared for the unexpected, because they rushed into operation before they were really ready, and because they assume that everything will just "work out for the best". Planning for the décor of the beautiful dining rooms was so well done, but planning for the fitness of the ship to sail with 2200 people aboard, was not well done. Shortcuts were made. What shortcuts have you made in your business? Good, thorough planning is essential. Keeping well informed about your business has no substitute. Do you know what your flow of money is, going out and coming in? Without such knowledge,your business can never hope to be sustainable.

The most fearsome battleship ever built in modern times was the Bismarck, operated by Nazi Germany in 1940. It had enormous power, with long range guns which rocked the ship every time they were fired. The builders knew that would happen, and compensation for that recoil was made. The first enemy target was the pride of the British fleet, the HMS Hood. The Bismarck found the Hood in the waters off Iceland, and engaged it. The first volley went far beyond the Hood. The second volley fell short of the Hood. The third volley was a direct hit, and the Hood sank with almost all hands aboard in a matter of minutes. The Bismarck then became the target of an all-out attempt to destroy it. Seemingly impervious to attack, the day came soon when a small torpedo plane hit it, but didn't sink it. Instead, the torpedo hit the rudder and froze it askew in one position. The mighty Bismarck, once so fearsome, was now locked into going in circles. It was unable to go back to occupied France. Soon, many torpedo planes reduced this 'sitting duck' to a smoking ruin and it sank with all hands-on board. It sank because it became helplessly vulnerable. What is your business vulnerable to? What could sink it? Are you frozen into one way of doing things, unwilling to change with the times? Have you identified your business' Achilles heel, and prepared for it? Is disruptive technology threatening your business? Are you still making horse drawn vehicles when the market is clearly moving to automobiles?

Are you insisting on making and selling cassettes, when better ways are obvious? Are you still selling land phones when the smartphone has taken over the market? Have you waited too long to get out? Don't go around and around in circles trying to figure this out. Do something!

Theory of Disruption

What will the competition do in response to what you do?

Give your customers something they can get nowhere else, not just something "better"

A car anyone can afford

Why have two such examples been used to illustrate the topic of business sustainability? Each began in a spectacular way with great expectations. Each was built and launched with the firm belief that they would succeed beyond anyone's imagination. No one would put so much into a project knowing it would fail. Yet, both are laying at the bottom of the same ocean, both on their maiden voyages, lasting only a short time out in the "real world" with no precautions taken to insure their sustainability.

New Customers

Eric Ries, in his fine book "The Lean Startup", describes sustainability as an 'engine of growth', and describes well where growth comes from. His proverb is ; **"New customers come from the actions of past customers"**

New customers drive new sales and new growth, and therefore sustainability. New customers come from four sources:

Word of mouth

Satisfied, excited customers telling others they know about you, your business, your products, your services and urging them to visit your business. What can you do in your business to make your customers enthusiastic about you? Look at the Mango Berry example on page 79. People came once or twice, were turned off and never went back! Sustainability: 2 years!

As a side effect of using your product: People look at what you are wearing, driving, eating, reading, making, and without even talking to you, want some too. The power of suggestion draws in new customers. Remember the Starbucks example (page 127)? There is another example in an East Coast chain of convenience stores known as Wawa. They are booming, adding new stores all the time. "Gotta have a Wawa!" is their trademark!

Advertising.

Irresistible, well done ads, placed on TV, hanging on posters, handed out to people, placed on Facebook and other electronic social media will draw new customers in. The MyPillow ads, done by the founder of that company, are a good example (see page 25). The originator of the Geico gecko with a British accent must be a wealthy person, as that image is worth millions.

Repeat purchasing.

Get your customers to keep coming back to you again and again. That will not happen if they deal with you and feel that they have been cheated. Even if your customers are tourists who come once and are never seen again, they must not be taken advantage of, as they are in many parts of the world. Word gets around. Good, fair treatment is rare, and when it happens, it is remembered. Bad treatment is not rare, and it is remembered too.

On page 126, the Charcoal Pit is mentioned as a business with fantastic sustainability. People like the product, the price and the way they are treated! That place has the same four-person booths it has had for 63 years! If you have a group of 5 people or more, you need to occupy two separate booths!! Competitors spring up around it, have their 'day in the sun', and die. President Obama visited the place because it is such an institution in the area. It isn't beautiful, but it is GOOD! You get your money's worth! They haven't changed the menu in decades!

Sustainability means 'staying up with the times'. It means "catching the wave" when it happens. One grocery store offers all organic food, charging a bit more than competitors, but selling to the millennial public who have heard about protecting their health since birth. This store chain is WholeFoods. It has recently been sold to Amazon because that giant company has an enormous distribution network and can now offer wholesome, organic food to customers who want home delivery! This is a good example of forward integration, leveraging a company's strengths to enlarge their business.

Another example of forward integration which did not work so well was the attempt by Pepsi Cola Company to own a chain of restaurants. Pepsi competes with Coca Cola Company for business in the fast food restaurants. Both vied for business with Pizza Hut, McDonald's, Burger King, KFC, Taco Bell and all the rest. Then PepsiCo decided to forward integrate into the fast food business, thus owning their customers. This effectively shut out Coca Cola from all those stores. This proved to be an unwise move because:

McDonald's now would have no choice but to buy Pepsi from what is now a rival fast food company. They immediately went to Coca Cola. The loss of business was devastating for Pepsi.

Pepsi now had to financially support and invest in thousands of fast food stores and do it with people who had little understanding of how that was done. Pepsi's core business was producing drink, not running restaurants. This put Pepsi in financial jeopardy. All the restaurants were a millstone around their neck!

Shortly, Pepsi had to stop the bleeding of money and sell all the stores. Then the challenge was to regain business from McDonald's and others they had "abandoned".

Will the lady in Nepal buy a chain of jewelry stores? Probably not.

Will the lady in Cote d'Ivoire buy a chain of clothing stores? This would not be a sustainable idea. Would she invest in her own cotton plantation? Not a good idea.

Will the man who made and sold chicha morada buy a chain of restaurants? He doesn't even know how to operate a restaurant. It would probably be a mistake.

Chapter 10 Business Ethics and Boundaries

Subject:	Business Ethics and Boundaries
Lesson Objectives:	To operate my business in a way which treats everyone in an ethical way so that they enjoy working with me and buying from me, and will pass the word to others who will become my customers too.
	To be certain that all who deal with me know that I love God and work ultimately for Him.
	To receive the ultimate reward for honoring God with my business by hearing His words "Well done, good and faithful servant".
Books Recommended	"Success God's Way", Dr. Charles Stanley
	The Bible, Old and New testaments

Introduction

What do we mean by "ethics" and why they are important?

What is the source of the "ethics" by which I will operate my business?

What is the danger to my business if I do not have a consistent set of core values or ethics? What happens when my business boundaries are not well drawn?

Ethics answers the question "what Is the right thing for me to do?"

Case Studies

Business ethics is a code of conduct, or behavior. Fresh out of college, I joined a large chemical firm which demonstrated a solid code of ethics from the morning I walked into the offices and laboratories. I was impressed by their emphasis on behavior influencing co-worker comradery as well as the good public opinion they wanted to build on. I was proud to work for that company for 37 years.

Ethics is described as a discipline which differentiates what is good and bad behavior. It is the framework which guides your and your employees' moral duty as prescribed by the business. Ultimately, the basis for such moral duty is the Bible, and as a "Kingdom Business", it is the Bible which is the guideline. In every business, in every part of the world, a company no matter how large or small, is faced with moral decisions. This chapter will deal with the most common areas in which we are tempted to cross the boundary of good behavior, and how we should react to such temptations.

Following are some of the guidelines set forth throughout history:

- "What you do not want done to yourself, do not do to others". Confucius
- "Treat others as you would have them treat you." Jesus
- "To lead people, you must walk beside them." Max Lucado
- "To see what is right and not do it, is cowardice." Confucius
- "A man who wants to lead the orchestra, must turn his back on the crowd" Max Lucado
- " A good name is better than great riches; to be esteemed is better than silver or gold." Proverbs in the Bible
- "A false balance is an abomination to the Lord" Proverbs 11:1

Does this work in practice? It does. Remember LYNAYS in Abidjan (page 59)? It is working well in a harsh environment. Chick-Fil-A is a Christian business selling chicken sandwiches. This company accumulates more profit per square foot of operating space than the McDonald's restaurant chain, and yet is only open 6 days per week, closing its doors every Sunday and encouraging its employees to attend a house of worship. Sunday is set aside to honor the Lord and is one of the company's core values.

High Ethical Behavior

Just As Safety Is Good Business, High Ethical Behavior Is Good Business Too!

You as the business owner should set the boundaries of behavior for yourself and each of your employees. Adhering to such must be a condition of employment without exception.

Following is a discussion of the most common areas in which our company morality is tested.

Corruption

Corruption is a blanket term covering many areas of misbehavior. It is rampant in most of the world, including the United States. Corruption takes different forms. The most common is giving people money for doing a job that they are already paid to do. Also common is demanding personal payment, using their power to hurt you if you don't comply. I many parts of the world, the police take advantage of people. Other people are put in positions of authority in which they are incompetent, but use those positions to demand payment and threaten to block your progress if you don't.

The 'Corruption pyramid" is common. Many levels of people operating in a "pyramid scheme", demand money from the victims and people up the line all get cuts of that payoff. Otherwise, your progress is severely hampered. Person A is in a position to set up a layer below them, give that layer a title, and the authority to demand graft or payoff before they sign approval. The position is needless and accomplishes nothing, but there they are, sitting in your way. The Person B in that sub-layer also has the authority to set up Person C, who claims to have authority to collect money, but in reality is useless to helping you to make progress in setting up your business. To them, time is of no matter at all. They often take a very cavalier attitude in how they treat you. This "performance" is a way of showing their power and authority, justifying their position. You

201

are told that you need Person C's approval. This person agrees to see you and sign your papers on Thursday. You come on time, with the proper papers, and the person waves you on, telling you to come back next week! Perhaps if some money is passed under the table, this could be "speeded up a bit". Part of that money goes up the line to person B, and to person A. Such behavior describes one of the most common forms of corruption. It is global! Disregard for the interests of others and greed for money is the driver. How will you handle that when you want to set up your own business? Do you place "graft and corruption payments" as a line item in your company cost sheet?

People place value in having received something extra, even if in reality, they didn't. In a coastal city of Kenya, Maersk ships arrive into port. Unloading is difficult unless you have an "agreement" with the longshoremen. The workers won't unload the boat until you agree to a bribe, which could consist of cigarettes and vodka. At the end of the week, however, you can deduct the value of these items from the total monetary payment. They just feel better that they received a bribe!

Business Ethics-right & wrong

Corruption or Bribes (Amos 5:12)

(Prov 11:1) Payoffs to get what you want

A restaurant chain wanted to open a number of stores in Moscow. In order to set up a reliable supply chain of all the foods which they offer, they had to first build a "Foodtown" factory on the outskirts of town. Otherwise, the supply would be very uncertain. You can't have a sandwich without bread! So the location was agreed upon, and Finnish workers were brought in to begin construction. As the large building became obvious, black limousines were seen circling the area. One day, someone got out of a limo to ask what was going on. Soon, another black limo stopped and the person approached the construction foreman and told him that he needed to pay for "protection". If he didn't pay for protection, he might see some of his labor force fail to show up for work in the coming days. Ignoring that threat didn't help. Day after day, some people didn't show up for work. It was decided to appeal to the mayor of the city. He demanded a share of the profits of the stores once they started in operation. The harassment and the threats, and the losses of workers, stopped immediately! This non-Christian company is in operation even to this day, 25 years later. How would you have handled this had you desired to open your business there?

Some equate graft payments with tips at a restaurant. Some claim that a "TIP" is an acronym for "To Insure Promptness". But they are quite different. A tip given to a person serving you is a reward for a job well done, after the fact. A "finder's fee" is similar. Graft and corruption is a threat preventing you from getting any service unless you pay them up front. A tip is always coupled with performance. Corruption payments are demanded with no connection to performance at all. A person earns a tip. A corrupt thief earns nothing, adds no value. Corruption comes in many varieties: extortion, blackmail, overcharging (like the tax collectors who worked for the Romans in the days of the new testament), embezzlement, skimming, unfair trade practices.

This huge, universal problem is basically sin, and we must learn to live with it until God changes hearts and one by one, it is diminished. So how do you, as a Christian entrepreneur or employee, learn to live with it? I can only offer advice.

Pray about it, and ask God to give you the stamina to endure it. As God has prompted you to start and run a business in a certain part of the world, you are a light in darkness and need to find God totally sufficient. Decide not to partake in sin, applying Romans 6:1,2, 11-14 to your life every day. Plan for tough and frustrating days. Never fail to explain to corrupt officials what you believe and why you just have to say "no" to threats. Apply I John 4:4 to your life.

You may have to put aside visions of grandeur for your business. Keep your business appearance smaller, rather than larger, so as not to appear on anyone's radar screen, if you live in a corruption prone area in which corruption is a way of life and is not punished by law authorities who are also corrupt. In many parts of this world, there are no "first responders" to come to your rescue should someone threaten you. It might be to your advantage to keep your enterprise in smaller parts.

Always do the basic things to keep an honest business and give no one the excuse to shut your business down because you broke the law in some way. Avoiding paying taxes is very common. Paying taxes should be in your plan, a line item in your cost sheet. It is not in many places of business, with the owners hoping that their business is so small that no one will ever notice. Conduct yourself in a way that causes no one to go out in your area talking against you. Garner favor with the community by going out of your way to treat them properly and fairly.

An old African proverb says "Don't do anything until It begins to smell really bad, then let It go". So If an employee, or a supplier, Is lying to you or cheating you, do nothing about it until you can't stand it anymore. A man stole $1000 from a missions fund in a church, and the pastor had to do something to show that he was pro-active. He decided the best thing to do was to tell him he couldn't take communion, to sit in the back row, and to tell him he wasn't permitted to tithe anymore. You see, he really wasn't such a bad person! Besides, some day I might need to steal from the church, and then no one will punish me! How do you control that mindset if these are your employees?

Another form of corruption is from within. We are told in Deuteronomy 4:16 to "beware lest you become corrupt." Do not be drawn away by your own successes, and stop giving thanks to God." Deut 4:19. Do not hold back, deciding the cheat the Lord. Don't ask "where have I cheated you Lord?" Malachi

Cronyism and nepotism

Cronyism

Hire and pay
Unqualified
People just
Because they
Are your friends

A man I know was working for 18 years for a reputable, Christian company in America. The company of 4000 employees was family owned. One day, his boss told him that one of his 7 responsibilities would be given to another person because he was quite overloaded, although still doing a good job. No problem! Soon, another one of his responsibilities was given to yet another person. Finally, this one man was replaced by 7 new people!! One of those 7 people proved to be so inept at his assignment that the company hired a consultant to help him. So in essence, this one employee was replaced by 8 new people, at far more cost than before. But no matter, because all of these people were related to the owner of the firm! That is nepotism. Giving jobs to family members or cronies just because they "need a job", not because they have earned it, or are more qualified. This is a vile way to run a business and is sure to reduce margins and will discourage the performance and loyalty of some employees. It may be morally acceptable, but it is not smart.

Business "Entertainment"

There is no law against it. It is easy to do. It's even tempting to do, and business people can "entertain" and win favors by doing it. However, taking your customers to see sexually explicit events and into places where this happens, is not setting an example of Christian behavior. To do it only once, can reduce public opinion of you and your business and make it easier to go in that direction over and over.

I was with a group in a large eastern European city, and after working a long day with an oil company, the group started out for a restaurant that had been recommended. I gladly walked with them to the place. Finding it was underneath a building, I walked down the stairs to discover a dimly lit, smoky "restaurant" with lewd women. I had to make a choice right away. To go in meant compromising my moral beliefs as a married, Christian man, and to leave meant a very long walk. I excused myself and made the walk; in a strange city, black, rainy night, seemingly miles back to the hotel. The next morning, I was well rested and felt great for another days work, and the others were not in great condition. Their stories didn't have much appeal.

Sometimes, you simply have to draw a line and adhere to it.

At other times, entertainment is offered and it is hard to turn down. Years ago, Japan's geisha girls were a "gift for the evening". I didn't ask for a geisha, or expect one, until we all met at a nice, Tokyo restaurant and I was presented with my geisha for the night. I didn't engage and soon, she was called away, and for a moment, I was relieved, only to find that she was replaced with someone else. My hosts thought I didn't like the first one, so they got another one. It was a nice experience, with good conversation, but it was unexpected.

If you are operating a company that claims to be owned by God, a "kingdom business", then the Bible gives us clear guidelines. I Thessalonians 5:22 "abstain from all appearance of evil", is just one of many verses. These instructions could be one of the core values of the company.

Sometimes, well-meaning colleagues can interest you in visiting a point of interest, which may interest them, but shouldn't interest you. In Stuttgart, Germany is the "Dreifarbenhaus" (house of three colors) and my friend told me it was of key historical interest. The name didn't make me suspicious, and I went. Upon walking in the front door, and beginning the walk down a long hall, it was quickly apparent that I was not in a museum, but in a house of ill repute! I kept walking, quickly! What exactly was the historical interest? I never found out. Just leave!

Exchanging personal favors (Pay for play)

I'll do this for you, if you do this for me. That's not illegal. It's just good trading, good bargaining, good business. But in some cases, it crosses the line. For example, your company has a large contract that needs to be given out to another company who can provide a service for you. Maybe it is to install a new computer software system for you because your old system isn't keeping up, or isn't fully capable of all that you need. Several companies are asked to quote and you see them, one by one. Some quotes are much higher than others, and the offerings are a bit different too, but all meet the criteria you asked for. You should use the lowest quote as long as all these criteria are met, and you are confident that the job will be done. However, one of the higher quote offers come from a company that will give you personal favors. "Give us the job and we will give you and your family tickets for deep sea fishing off the coast of the Bahamas". Your company suffers higher cost, but you get a gift! You are not concerned about what your company has to pay for the project, but just hope you don't get caught if someone examines all the bids and sees that you have accepted a higher one. Tickets for you and your family to attend the masters golf tournament in Augusta, Georgia cannot be a basis for awarding a company contract. Such behavior should be a condition for termination of the person's job.

False Intentions and Misrepresentation

Borrowing money with no intention of paying it back

You lie about your intention

Obtaining money for one purpose with no intention of using it for that purpose but instead using it for something quite different (or worse, for personal reasons). Claiming to have a definite need, and in reality not having such a need and using that claim to obtain information for another entity. What do you think of someone who agrees, signs the papers, takes the money and forgets what they agreed to? Dishonest, untrustworthy and even criminal.

In the introduction, some customs in certain parts of the world make this a problem. I want to start a business in my hometown making shirts, and get enough money from a local bank. I find that my mother has a sudden medical need and the bank's money in my pocket will cover that need. I have failed to understand that it is not my money; it belongs to the bank. They have loaned it to me for a specific purpose and they expect to be paid back! What do I tell the bank when they call for the return of their money?

In Liberia, I teach courses, and use a projector for PowerPoints. I am tired of projecting against a wooden wall, so I buy a screen which can be used for anyone who wants to come and teach. It becomes the property of the school, as a gift from me. The next time I return to teach, I ask for the screen I bought and gave, and...it's gone. Where did it go? It is explained to me that the screen was given to another person who said he needed it. That's fine, so let's go get it back! It is explained to me that we can't do that now, because he moved a long distance away and took it with him. We call the man, and get the news: he sold it; he needed the money because he had an accident with his motorbike and had to buy a new one. Unchristian thoughts race through my mind.

To me, this speaks of misrepresentation, dishonesty, false intentions. The recipient of the screen originally said "thank you, we need this in our school", but when no one was using it, readily gave it to another person. Even that sounds natural enough, but to not be responsible to have it for it's understood purpose is hard for persons of another culture to comprehend. The problem here is the understanding of ownership. To the western mind, ownership is sacred. Taking something that belongs to another is theft. In other cultures, it is understood that if it isn't being needed at the time, and if I need it, I can take it. It wasn't being used! I can use any excuse to take it, even telling a lie if need be.

How can a business employ such people and hope to survive? Clear communication of allowable behavior is needed by the business owner.

Sexual Harassment

Unwanted, unsolicited "help and friendship" from one colleague to another, for the intended purpose of sexual advancements or services is improper in any place of business. It should be clearly understood by every employee that such is grounds for termination of employment. This has to be backed up by factual data and proof, of course. If such a problem occurs inside your business, then it requires a formal inquiry and then needs to be quickly addressed and resolved, not allowed to go on for long periods of time. Your business' reputation is at stake.

False Advertising

You asked for two bananas

Often called Bait & Switch

I gave you one Pineapple

False Advertising

This is the well-known "bait and switch" tactic, of promising one thing and getting paid for it, and then delivering something else. Suppose your business is approached by a supplier that makes up your supply chain, and a purchase is made. When the goods come and they are something quite different, you of course have to make that known and ask for a rebate and/or have the correct items shipped at the suppliers expense. A reputable company will gladly do that because they want to keep your business and please you. Any company that will not honor their commitment to fulfill your orders should be dropped and replaced.

One set of books, or two?
To pay taxes or not to pay taxes?

 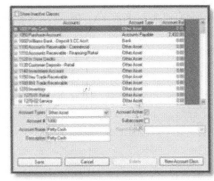

Companies and individuals keep a sets of books based on false invoices and false records which they can show the revenue of the government if ever called up to do that. That happens in the USA and in all other countries. Sometimes the company will show to a revenue auditor the true report and for a certain amount of money, the auditor will issue a false report to his own employer (could even be the government) and report that. It's considered "getting milk for his babies". Some larger companies in Peru and many other places have a "tax planning division", to put the company in the best position with the tax collectors. Is that really any different than H&R Block, who can try to save you money on your taxes? In principle, no. As a Christian company, your business should be honest as possible, to be above reproach, and to plan ahead for the proper paying of taxes.

Control of anger and other forms of abuse, including drugs & alcohol

Does this man leave a good impression of what a Christian is like?

Control of Anger and other forms of abuse.

In some cultures, open expression of anger is a form of control that the "boss" should have. In Japan, some executives are sent to training camp in the mountains to practice screaming, with clenched fists! In other cultures, the managers and directors, or the owners, are intentionally late for meetings. Perhaps you show up on time, then those who may be at your level show up, and sit around a table, but all is silent except for coffee service and small talk, until…the boss comes in. This may be an hour later! The later, the better. Being on time would show that the boss doesn't have much to do. Being late is an indication of how important he is. And of course, the meeting can't meaningfully start without his vital presence. This is abuse of your time, and it is practiced a lot. Expressions of anger are usually reserved until after the meeting when the customer is gone, and then the employees are the victims.

The idea that anger and screaming at people is a way to drive them into proper behavior and to assure results, is wrong. A Christian employer from top to bottom needs to treat others as they themselves wish to be treated, with honor and respect. This is Jesus' teaching (Luke 6:31). Good behavior at the workplace needs to be modeled and expected. If it isn't happening, that employee needs counseling. There is never an excuse for loss of temper and mental (or physical) abuse.

What kind of impression do you have of people who cannot control themselves? Would you want to give 100% effort to such a person? Is that what a Christian looks like? If such a person talks with you about faith in Christ, do you believe him?

Reputation of being cheap, stingy & rude.
You can cheat a customer only once! Then the word about you is spread

A good reputation is like gold, precious and often hard to find. A good reputation takes years to build and one moment to destroy!

You can cheat a customer one time, and then the word spreads that you are dishonest, cheap or rude. Maintaining your good reputation is like driving a car...always look where you are going, and check where you have been. Gypping customers has already been discussed. Those who treat customers that way, will never win for long. Seeing people like that go out of business is almost a pleasure. My model was my father, a self-employed salesman, who did anything possible to make his customers happy. He treated them fairly, and was regarded as an "honest man".

The one Bible character who exhibited honesty all of his life was Joseph (Genesis 36-50). Tested often, with being in a pit, abandoned by his brothers who staged his death, tested by Potiphar's wife, and again by pharaoh, and finally by his brothers who after so many years didn't recognize him, Joseph never wavered in his faith in the one true God. He was God's friend, and God never let him down. Sometimes, Joseph felt abandoned by God, then realized he was being used by God. You will feel this way in business too. Sometimes, you will be alone, a bit betrayed, asking God how He would allow this to happen. But God is faithful. Maintain a good reputation of being true to the calling that God has given you to operate a business His way! Light always dispels darkness, never the other way around. People will see the difference in you and your business!

Conclusion

Does having a consistent set of ethics, or a code by which I operate my business, make sense or not? As for me and my business, it does make sense and God blesses that.

What is the right thing, in my gut, that I should do?

214

Chapter 11 Characteristics of a Successful Business Person

Subject:	Characteristics of a Successful Business Person
Lesson Objectives:	To present a simple list outlining the character of a successful business person, anywhere in the world.
Books Recommended	"Kiss, Bow or Shake Hands", Morrison, Conaway, Borden "Success God's Way", Dr. Charles Stanley

Introduction

This section is meant to be a template for a talk given on the subject of this book. Each of these things are viewed differently in various parts of the world. To use an extreme example, there are people of the Baleem Valley of Irian Jaya, who have an entirely different regard for honesty. They cannot be called "dishonest", but they are indeed different. When a man visited these people in 1954 to share the Bible stories with them, they were quite bored...until...the teacher began to describe Judas! They LOVED Judas, who had betrayed Jesus. They howled with delight at Judas' accomplishment. The reason became evident when the man was invited up to a tree house one day for dinner. He had achieved a level of language proficiency, and felt he had built up a rapport with them too. He was aiming at a relationship of trust. But this time, he had a sense of foreboding. He was not being invited to have dinner with them; he WAS the dinner with these cannibals. He looked for an opportunity to leap off the platform and run for his life. With spears and arrows narrowly missing him as he set speed records down through the dense jungle, he dove into a river and using a reed through which to breathe, remained undiscovered for 24 hours.

These people placed a high value on their ability to deceive. They almost succeeded!

While the setting may be totally different in most other parts of the world, the objective isn't.

Carefully considering the culture of the audience, use this list of characteristics of a successful business person to help them build a more satisfying business.

Steps to Success

INTEGRITY AND HONESTY-refuse to be dishonest

PLAN WELL-do a good business plan

HARD WORK AND DEDICATION-be available for your customers

KNOW WHEN TO ENTER A BUSINESS AND WHEN TO EXIT-keep up with the times

TREAT OTHERS AS YOU WOULD LIKE TO BE TREATED

- Your coworkers
- Your customers
- Your employees

LEARN HOW TO ESTIMATE WELL-do good research, fact checking

SEEK GOOD ADVICE-always ask questions of those you know and trust

THINK AHEAD OF THE CURVE. BE READY WHEN OTHERS ARE NOT.

STAY WITH WHAT YOU DO WELL, AND NOT DO BUSINESS YOU KNOW NOTHING ABOUT-stay within your comfort zone.

EARN A GOOD REPUTATION, VALUE IT AND KEEP IT-hard to build up; can be ruined in a moment of time.

TRAIN LEADERS TO TAKE YOUR PLACE SOMEDAY-all of the knowhow cannot reside in just you.

HAVE A CLEAR SET OF BUSINESS ETHICS IN MIND

BE RESILIENT-you will have difficult days; learn to bounce back.

WHAT'S IN IT FOR ME, VERSUS WHAT'S IN IT FOR MY CUSTOMER? Remember that the customer is always first.

DON'T CHEAT. IT WILL ONLY WORK ONCE.-you will never succeed for long by cheating. Deceiving others is not a workable strategy.

SUCCESSFUL PEOPLE DON'T FEEL BADLY ABOUT MAKING MONEY; IT DOESN'T BELONG TO THEM ANYWAY; IT BELONGS TO GOD.

- Psalm 24: "The earth is the Lord's"
- Psalm 67:1-7 "Give so you'll be blessed"
- Psalm 90:17 "Pray to establish your work
- Luke 16:10 and Matthew 25:29 "If you are faithful with a little, you will be made ruler over much"

HAVE A CLEAR VISION OF WHERE THE COMPANY SHOULD GO-pay close attention to sustainability.

COMMUNICATE THAT VISION WELL TO OTHERS-include others in your orbit of business activities, and make roles and responsibilities clear

BE CAPITALIZED BEFORE YOU BEGIN. You need money to make money. Borrow as little as possible, or you will be a slave to the lender. As part of your monthly and yearly business practice, set aside money to be used only for one thing: to further or expand the business, to buy that third sewing machine, etc. Learn to become self-financed in each form of capital expenditure.

Chapter 12 The Importance of SAFETY

Subject:	Safety
Lesson Objectives:	To make your business workplace a safe place for all and with no business interruptions
Books Recommended	Numerous articles from "Plant Engineering" and "Chemical Processing" magazines, and a lot of personal experience

Introduction

Keeping your workplace operation and environment safe from harm to your assets and your employees and customers is simply GOOD BUSINESS! Safety on the job is a form of sustaining your business and keeping it free from interruption. Equally important, good safety practices train people for both on the job and off the job protection from accidents, injuries and death. Safety practices prove that you CARE. Well cared for employees will give you as the owner more attention and do a better job.

Safety is good business because it assures your customers that you will STAY in business and not have to call a halt to your products and services because of damage caused by carelessness. What will your customers do if you put out the news that your place will be "out of operation" for 6 months while you make repairs from a fire? They will go elsewhere, and probably not come back. You can't afford loss of customers, income, and all the extra expense that comes with cleaning up after a safety mishap. You can't afford the reputation killer that someone died as a result of working for you.

Don't have a day when you must visit a family and tell them that their husband or wife will not be coming home again.

Elements of a safe operation.

Good quality, well maintained equipment (could be a sewing machine, a coffee maker, a shoe repair shop, a plastics recycling facility or a palm oil processing facility)

Regular safety inspections, carried out by the personnel who have to work there, rather than outside agencies.

Regularly scheduled, monthly safety meetings, assigning rotating leadership of such meetings to members of your organization.

Well understood, clear safety instructions as part of the overall training of personnel in your operation. A member of your organization should have the role of managing safety indoctrination to other members of the staff.

Reminders posted in prominent places, such as:

- The Goal is Zero (injuries, fatalities, incidents)
- PAR (personal acceptance of responsibility)
- STOP (If you can't do it safely, don't do it)
- LOCK, TAG &TRY (before you try to make serious repairs, shut it down and lock it out, so another person cannot inadvertently throw the switch and start it up.
- See something ; Say something! Call attention to something which looks suspicious in machine or personnel behavior, before an accident happens!

As the owner or manager of the business, you must decide the boundaries of each of these facets of safety. You must decide who should be the "local expert" in taking care that the best equipment is installed, that people know how to operate it and that training is transferred from one to another as job assignments change. Here are some typical points of attention:

- Fire extinguishers: are there enough, in the right place, for the right purpose (oil fire, electrical fire, other combustibles)? Are people trained to use them on quick notice?
- Sprinkler system: has it been installed properly and does it work when needed?
- Phone numbers: are the correct emergency phone numbers well posted?
- Are flammables properly stored and not close to one another in case there is an ignition?
- Are the air vent systems kept clean, and not a source of a fire which is hard to reach and difficult to put out before a lot of damage is done?
- Are necessary medical supplies available in case some needs attention quickly?

While certain types of businesses don't require a detailed safety analysis, there are some which do, by nature. For example, a palm oil processing plant, or the equipment invented by the girls in Nigeria or the reduction to fuel in Japan are well suited for a Failure Mode & Effect Analysis. With every component of the operating equipment, ask yourself what could fail, how could it fail, and if it did fail, what would be the effect? What is the probability that it would fail as you have described it? If something could likely fail, and if it did fail, would the results be disastrous (building burn down, someone electrocuted, etc), then take immediate steps to repair it.

Finally, you as the owner should practice "Preventative Maintenance". Some well-meaning people dig water wells for those who live in remote areas and provide clean water for them to use for the first time in their lives. This makes the donors feel great about what they have done, and indeed, it IS great! But there is seldom training on how to recognize that the equipment will eventually break down and will need repair. Instead, when an essential part gets stolen or the pump stops working for lack of maintenance, the people return to using the same dirty water they have used for centuries. Animals stand in the same water the people drink from! Health safety was provided by this effort, but when it stops, it is no longer safe. Regardless of the endeavor you are doing, attention needs to be paid to preventing breakdowns. People need to be trained what to look for before the breakdown happens. Perhaps lubricating the moving parts might help? Would a regular six-month inspection, with replacement of worn parts help? Would having this as a planned, scheduled event help? Preventing a failure doesn't cost very much: breakdown of the equipment does!

Personal protective equipment seems obvious in some parts of the world, but not in all. In India, for example, a construction site hires many kinds of skilled and unskilled labor. Electricians, pipefitters, block layers, equipment drivers, etc all bring their families to live with them, often right on the construction site! Bricks are falling, ladders are erected, improper tools are used and many other dangerous practices, with people wearing minimum because it is so hot, and no shoes at all, no gloves, no glasses, and no hardhats! Trying to insist on proper PPE is nearly impossible. The family of the worker is often cooking, sleeping and playing right under the work zone. Provide your entire staff with the necessary PPE!

Epilogue

One morning in Iquitos, Peru I met a man who changed my way of thinking more than he will ever know. I was in this hot, humid city on the Amazon River to give a two-day lecture to about 100 pastors and workers. These people came from all parts of the Amazon jungle. Their journey to get to this meeting place was not easy, as there are no roads for cars in and out of Iquitos; only river craft and an airport. I began my talk, using a microphone and a translator, at 9AM. Shortly after we began, a man walked into the rear of the auditorium and walked slowly down the aisle, carrying only a Bible, a notebook and a pencil. He walked unassisted. He sat right in front of me and began to listen and take notes. I was busy talking, but could not help but notice that he was quite old. Curiosity mounted in me as he sat there taking notes, and at the first break, I stepped forward to introduce myself and ask him his name and how old he was. "My name is Manuel, and I am 100 years old." He smiled as he looked at me, 40 years his junior.

Others verified that he was indeed that old, and my wife later gave him a medical exam in a make-shift clinic. He was born in 1900, and at age 35, had given his heart to Christ. For the last 65 years, he had served as a pastor to 5 churches. Each one of these churches was located one of the many tributaries which feed the Amazon. Manuel could only reach each one of them by canoe. He served each day of the week, talking with his parishioners, praying with them and doing other 'pastor' things.

It is my desire, God willing, to be a faithful man like Manuel. I want to still be going to seminars, learning new things, taking notes, and sharing what I learn with others. It is my hope that you will do likewise, as God has called you to be a Christian business person in a dark world. May God's welcoming words be, as we enter into His presence someday, "Well done, my good and faithful servant'!

I returned a year later. He was gone. Never be discouraged. Never give up!

The Baobab tree of Senegal lending it's shade and care to many younger Baobab trees. This book was written in the same spirit by passing on my experience to others. If you want more information or discussion contact me at esrowse@verizon.net
The Power Point presentation is available for a small cost.

Bibliography

The Bible, both old and new testaments

"The Lean Start-up", Eric Ries

"EntreLeadership", Dave Ramsey

"Complete Guide to Money", Dave Ramsey

Numerous magazine articles, such as Business Week, Plastics News, Rubber News, etc.

"The Everything Business Plan Book", Dan Ramsey and Stephen Windhaus

Semester of Business Planning, given at the Delaware Technological College, February, 2013

Nearly 55 years of personal, worldwide business experience as a professional engineer engaged in business start ups

Discussions with Kent R. Wilson, WorldVenture, in mid-2012

"Top Ten Reasons Why Businesses Fail", Jay Goltz in "The Thinking Entrepreneur".

"The E-myth, revisited" , Michael E. Gerber

"Leadership Coaching", Tony Stoltzfus

"Success God's Way", Dr. Charles Stanley

"Fundamentals of Corporate Finance", Brealey, Myers, Marcus

"Kiss, Bow or Shake Hands, how to do business in sixty countries", Morrison, Conaway and Borden

"Disruptive Technologies: Catching the Wave", Christensen and Bower, 1995

"The Innovator's Dilemma", Dr. Clayton Christensen

"God Owns my Business", Dr. Stanley Tam

"Cultures and Organizations", Geert Hofstede, Geert Jan Hofstede, Michael Minkov

"Fierce Conversations", Susan Scott

Made in the USA
Lexington, KY
23 November 2019